The Pursuit of Happiness

Peter Quennell

The Pursuit of Happiness

Little, Brown and Company

Boston   Toronto   London

Library of Congress Cataloging-in-Publication Data

Quennell, Peter, 1905–
    The pursuit of happiness/Peter Quennell. — 1st American ed.
        p.   cm.
    ISBN 0-316-72895-0
    1. Happiness in literature.   2. Literature — History and criticism.
3. Happiness in art.   I. Title.
PN56.H27Q46   1988
809'.93353 — dc19   88-13497
                                                                        CIP

10   9   8   7   6   5   4   3   2   1

HC

Published simultaneously in Canada
by Little, Brown & Company (Canada) Limited

PRINTED IN THE UNITED STATES OF AMERICA

To Alexander Quennell

Contents

Illustrations

ILLUSTRATIONS

I

Past and Present

THE origins of almost every book lie hidden somewhere in the writer's past; and my concern with happiness I can certainly trace back to an early period of my childhood. I had then an introspective and vaguely meditative turn that puzzled or annoyed my elders; and I recollect how, many years before I had heard of the great Spanish dramatist Calderon de la Barca, who once chose the haunting sentence '*Life is a dream*' as the title of a play, I was occasionally troubled by the fear that my own pleasant daily routine might prove to be a baseless vision, and that I should presently wake up to find myself in far gloomier surroundings.

I also questioned the real significance of familiar words and phrases. 'Happy', for example. What did 'happiness' mean? Was I happy, and were my parents happy? True, my mother now and then looked sad; she had a nervous disposition. But my father, I long believed, despite all the reverses he had suffered since the outbreak of the First World War, led a cheerfully courageous life, until one day, having just received before breakfast a letter from an admiring female correspondent in which she congratulated him on the splendid work he did, and referred to the happiness he and his wife must enjoy writing and illustrating side by side, he suddenly remarked 'Well, we're *not* happy, are we?' with an expression of profound despair.

The mood soon passed; and, seeing that my mother was both hurt and astonished, he hastened to make affectionate amends. But I never forgot the episode. My father was no Romantic, at least in the accepted literary sense; nor was he a self-tormenting melancholic. He preferred facts to feelings, solid, finely-built objects to ideas or intellectual theories. He

[11]

fought off doubts that threatened his peace of mind, regarded human happiness, I think, as the legitimate reward of a decent, ordinary career – those two last adjectives, by the way, in his vocabulary were terms of warm approval – and would have refused to admit that the condition called 'being happy' was a rare, mysterious privilege, not necessarily bestowed on virtue, or that its pursuit – frequently a vain pursuit – had perplexed and fascinated imaginative artists for the last two thousand years.

Yet even my father, I remembered, had suffered a momentary pang of doubt; and in later life I have sometimes urged my friends to discuss their personal views of this strange, entrancing state, and asked them how often they could claim that they had unmistakably experienced it. Their answers varied. While some spoke of happiness as a welcome yet always wayward visitor, which unpredictably descended and no less rapidly departed, others told of brief luminous moments, when they had not only been happy but had *known* they were happy and delighted in the knowledge; when, moreover, they had felt so much at peace with themselves, and by extension with the whole universe, that, like Jean-Jacques Rousseau on the Ile Saint-Pierre, they had seemed to soar beyond the reach of Time.

After consulting my friends, I next applied for help to historians and lexicographers. The idea of happiness, I was reminded, had had a very long history; the meaning of the words had slowly changed and each metamorphosis had reflected the changing climate of a different social epoch. In the Middle Ages and the Elizabethan heyday, it signified primarily 'good-hap', otherwise good luck, or the fortunate realisation of some personal design. That was its Shakespearian connotation:

> 'Wish me partaker in thy happiness
> When thou dost meet good hap'

exclaims Proteus, one of the *Two Gentlemen of Verona*, bidding Valentine farewell; and, as the description of a human quality, it was used to mean 'apt', 'appropriate', 'well-suited', or conveyed an air of physical accomplishment. 'He hath indeed a good outward happiness' says Don Pedro in *Much Ado about Nothing* of the highly personable Benedick.

Underlying most early uses of the word we can usually detect the assumption that happiness is a by-product of worldly success, gained either by heroic endeavour or by some brilliant stroke of fortune. Then, during the seventeenth century, it gradually acquired a far subtler and more interesting significance, and began to denote not so much a man's prosperous condition as an harmonious or exalted frame of mind. But it still possessed a double value; and, towards the end of the century, in the grandiose valedictory speech that John Dryden gave to the hero of his blank-verse tragedy *All for Love*, where Mark Antony reviews his squandered life, both shades of meaning are apparently combined:

> 'I was so great, so happy, so belov'd,
> Fate could not ruin me; till I took pains
> And work'd against my fortune, chid her from me . . .
> My careless days and my luxurious nights
> At length have wearied her, and now she's gone,
> Gone, gone, divorced for ever.'

Does Antony, the reader may well ask, most regret the joys of his temporal or those of his emotional existence – the belief that Cleopatra loves him, or the knowledge that he has conquered half the Roman world? Dryden, dictator of literary taste, dramatist and melodious lyricist, died in the first year of the next century; and his throne was rightly occupied by his heir presumptive Alexander Pope, who, between 1733 and 1734, published his ambitious *Essay on Man*, and opened its fourth section with a bold 'address to Happiness', which hails the emotion that it applauds, but cannot precisely define, as a 'seed' that has been dropped from heaven:

> 'Oh Happiness! our being's end and aim!
> Good, Pleasure, Ease, Content! Whate'er thy name:
> That something still which prompts th'eternal sigh,
> For which we bear to live, or dare to die . . .'

Once accepted, and fixed in memorable lines, by an Augustan master-poet, the idea rapidly extended its scope; and this book is an attempt to follow the subsequent pursuit of happiness as it has been recorded by creative

artists, and has affected the works and lives of individual men and women. Happiness is clearly multiform. The Greeks coined some six nouns to describe it (of which *eudaimonia* was the word that Aristotle used) and an equal number to denote the supplementary emotion joy, ranging from '*hédoné*', sensuous delight, to '*epicharma*', quietly malicious fun. By comparison, the resources of English and French – 'happiness' and '*bonheur*' developed simultaneously – are a great deal more limited. Yet, in each country, a literature has grown up that depicts every stage of the pursuit, and touches on innumerable aspects of the contemporary human scene. Here an interesting fact emerges. Although a host of strangely different writers have studied the subject, they appear to have reached, now and then, remarkably similar conclusions. Looking back to the past, they tell us, or gazing ahead towards the hopeful future, is always a far happier exercise than looking around us at the present day; and among those who have held that view are a particularly incongruous pair, Samuel Johnson in the Georgian Age and Ivan Turgenev in the nineteenth century.

On English eighteenth-century roads, for a man who did not own a carriage and shunned the discomforts of a public coach, to hire a post-chaise, which usually carried only two passengers, was the most expensive, but also the pleasantest, speediest and most fashionable mode of travelling. In 1776, Johnson, then aged sixty-seven, employed a chaise to carry him home from the North with his favourite disciple James Boswell; and Boswell, who always 'enjoyed the luxury of our approach to London, that metropolis which we both loved so much for the high and intellectual pleasure which it furnishes', and who 'experienced immediate happiness while whirled along with such a companion', referred to a provocative remark that, several months earlier, he had heard his venerable friend throw off, and that had apparently been troubling him. '. . . The present', Johnson had then asserted, 'was never a happy state to any human being', and, 'when he was pressed . . . and asked if he was really of opinion, that though, in general, happiness was very rare in human life, a man was not sometimes happy in the moment that was present, he answered, "Never but when he is drunk." '

Although Johnson was usually displeased to hear his dogmatic assertions questioned, in the ebullient mood their approach to London awoke Boswell was brave enough to risk a snub. 'Sir', he began, 'you observed one day at General Oglethorpe's, that a man is never happy for the present, but when he is drunk. Will you not add, – or when he is driving rapidly in a post-chaise?' 'No, Sir', Johnson replied, 'you are driving *from* something, or *to* something!' For all its outward acerbity, Johnson's character had a sympathetic and good-humoured side; and later he admitted that more than once he had himself felt extremely happy travelling in a post-chaise with a pretty woman. These light-hearted moments, he wished his audience to understand, had been comparatively rare; for, on his way through life, his spiritual and physical infirmities had 'seldom afforded him a single day of ease'. Yet, as a philosopher, he blamed despondency in others. 'The business of the wise man is to be happy', he informed the manic-depressive Boswell; and, on another occasion, having recommended that they should both of them do their best to be happy, he warned him against indulging in what he called the 'hypocrisy of misery' and the 'affectation of distress'.

He would not deny that even his uneasy life had had its memorable compensations. Some time after he had settled down at Streatham among his kindly friends the Thrales – Hester Thrale, his beloved 'mistress', and her dignified, substantial husband – Mr Thrale, always fond of hearing their guests talk, enquired 'which had been the happiest period of his life'; and he answered 'it was that year in which he spent one whole evening with Molly Aston. "That indeed (said he) was not happiness; it was rapture..." ' Again at Streatham, discussing *Evelina*, Fanny Burney's recently published novel, he reverted to the theme. Miss Burney's book, he said, 'concludes by leaving her heroine in measureless delight'; and he wondered 'when anybody ever experiences measureless delight', adding that he felt sure that he himself had never done so, since the unforgettable hours he had passed in Molly Aston's company.

Their meeting, of course, had been long ago, about the year 1739, at his humdrum birthplace, Lichfield; and, though to the Thrales he spoke of a 'Teste-a-Teste', he and Molly were certainly not alone; nor could Johnson, the impoverished thirty-year-old son of a bookseller who sometimes set up a stall in Lichfield market, have expected he might win the heart of a rich baronet's unmarried daughter. By that time he had already a middle-aged

consort, the difficult, exacting Tetty; and he was far too stern a moralist, his early biographer assures us, to cause his wife the smallest chagrin. Miss Aston, incidentally, professed the kind of opinions that in a woman, whatever her appearance and age might be, as a rule he most detested. A sharp-eyed, lively-looking girl with a handsome aquiline profile, she was 'a scholar, and a wit and a Whig' – Johnson, of course, supported the opposite camp – and during their conversation, she 'talked all in praise of liberty!' But his heart had overcome his political prejudices; 'she was the loveliest creature he ever saw!!!' he exclaimed; and Molly's face haunted his imagination so long as he still clung to life.

Boswell's biography is one of those masterpieces which, besides generously enlarging our knowledge of the world, strengthen our respect for human nature. Its hero, perverse, wrong-headed, downright brutal though he may often appear, had a strong attachment to his fellow men; they were his chief 'subject of enquiry', in which he never lost interest; like the Roman playwright, he thought nothing human entirely alien to himself. Another well-known book that provides a yet more extensive, and even more carefully detailed picture of a vanished social epoch, the *Journal* kept by Edmond and Jules de Goncourt, and, long after his brother's death, completed by Edmond in the year 1896, has precisely the opposite effect upon a critic's mind. Only the Goncourts – two unselfishly devoted artists; or so they very often announced – are usually portrayed as '*hommes de bonne volonté*'. Otherwise few of their distinguished colleagues escape some damaging strokes either of private malice or of literary spite. But an exception was Ivan Turgenev, perhaps because he was an interesting newcomer from a romantic foreign land, and also partly, no doubt, because he had an air of natural good breeding – the Goncourts regarded themselves as aristocrats – that George Moore, in his old age at Ebury Street, when he recollected the famous writers he had known, would affectionately describe.

Reopening the Goncourts' *Journal*, I alighted on two passages I had previously half forgotten, that reminded me of Johnson's tribute to the loveliest creature he had even seen, and of the part that Molly Aston had played in his sentimental education. The first entry was dated March 2nd 1872, and recorded a Parisian dinner-party that included Flaubert,

Molly Aston, the handsome young woman, 'a scholar, and a wit and a Whig', in whose company Johnson once experienced 'measureless delight'.

Théophile Gautier and their friend the Russian novelist – 'a good-natured giant . . . his white hair descending over his eyes', a deep wrinkle, 'deep as a cart-track', crossing his large brow from one temple to another. Flaubert and Edmond de Goncourt having denied that love was supremely important for a writer, Turgenev contradicted them. All he could say, he declared, was that his whole life had been 'saturated with femininity'; that there 'wasn't a book, or anything else, that could replace a woman for him'; and he believed that love produced a certain 'flowering of the personality', or expansion of the spirit, that no other influence could quite achieve.

Then his memory began to dig into the past; and 'a flash of happiness' lit up the giant's eyes. When he was a young man, he said, he had known a girl whom he often visited and made love to if he went out shooting, the child of a miller near St. Petersburg, a delightful being, very pale, with a cast in one eye, which, he explained, was fairly common among Russian women. She had never asked him for a present, until she suddenly admitted that there was indeed something she would like to have. 'Bring me some scented soap', she begged. He had brought it; and she had taken it, vanished, and come back rosy with emotion, holding out her fragrant hands. 'Now kiss them', she exclaimed, 'as you kiss the hands of the ladies in the drawing-rooms at St. Petersburg!' He had thrown himself on to his knees before her. There hadn't been another moment of his life, he concluded, that had given him so deep a joy.

The second passage I found was dated January 28th 1878, and is possibly yet more significant, since it illustrates not only Turgenev's conception of remembered happiness, but the masochistic strain, derived presumably from his painful relationship with his crazily oppressive mother, that may afterwards have dictated his long patient devotion to his one-time mistress Pauline Viardot. At a later dinner-party, he was prompted by his fellow-guests to tell them what had been his keenest amorous sensations; and he replied that, while he was young and innocent, with all the restlessness of a fifteen-year-old boy, and was wandering around the garden of his mother's country house on a damp, dull, rainy day – 'one of those erotic days' – her maid, who had a pretty stupid face, but the type of face that 'stupidity lends a certain grandeur', had walked straight up to him and, although (his companions must bear in mind) he was the master, and she a

mere serf, had grasped the locks at the nape of his neck, saying simply 'Come!' That gentle grasp sometimes returned to him; 'and just thinking about it makes me happy!'

The idea of happiness in retrospect clearly fascinated Turgenev; for a somewhat similar incident is recorded by Sergei Tolstoy among his reminiscences of his father's household.* During August 1881 Turgenev visited Yasnaya Polyana; and there a conversation took place that might very well, the younger Tolstoy remarks, have been an episode from one of his own stories. Somebody had 'raised the question as to which were the happiest moments of one's life'; and, while another guest, the high-minded local vice-governor, said that for him such a moment would have occurred had he learned of the ultimate triumph of Good-Will on earth, Turgenev admitted that, in his personal experience, happiness had always reached him through a woman's love, when at last you met the beloved's gaze and knew that she returned your passion, adding, after a brief reflective silence: 'This I experienced once in the course of my life – perhaps twice!' The declaration seemed to warm his heart; and, on the same visit, he amused the juvenile Tolstoys by demonstrating how to dance the French cancan. But he presently slipped and fell, and, although he picked himself up again with the agility of youth, his behaviour did not please Tolstoy, who noted that day on a page of his journal, '*Turgenev – cancan. Very sad.*'

After Turgenev's death, Pauline Viardot remarked that he was the unhappiest man, '*l'homme le plus triste*', she had ever known. Although this odd remark may have included a touch of feminine exaggeration – his fellow writers thought him good company; in his domestic life Madame Viardot's tyrannical treatment of him, once he had ceased to be her lover, probably weighed down his spirits – it is evident that, like Johnson, he had inherited a melancholic strain, from which he sought an emotional relief by looking back towards the past. But a conviction that happiness belongs to the past recurs again and again in literary self-revelations, where Memory selects a single fragment of experience, and then revives and recreates that period as an earthly paradise. Byron, for example, had found such a paradise, he afterwards believed, at his English public school; Harrow had brought him the admiration and the real affection that he had always lacked at home. 'My school friendships', he recorded in 1821 during a

* *Tolstoy Remembered*; translated by Moura Budberg, 1961.

[19]

latter stage of his Italian exile, 'were with *me passions* . . . that with Lord Clare began one of the earliest and lasted longest . . . I never hear the word "*Clare*" without a beating of the heart even *now* . . .'

In 1809, when Byron was about to set forth on his eastern Grand Tour, there had been a brief estrangement. He had suggested they should spend an hour together; and Clare had excused himself because, he said, he had promised 'his mother and some ladies' to take them out shopping. Yet, long afterwards, Byron had sighted his school-friend's carriage, while they travelled in opposite directions along an Italian high road; and they had dismounted, shaken hands and talked:

> 'This meeting annihilated for a moment all the years between the present time and the days of *Harrow*. It was a new and inexplicable feeling, like rising from the grave to me. Clare, too, was much agitated – *more* in appearance than even myself; for I could feel his heart beat to his fingers' ends, unless, indeed, it was the pulse of my own which made me think so – We were but five minutes together, and in the public road; but I hardly recollect an hour of my existence which could be weighed against them'

Luckily perhaps, we were few of us quite so happy either in our childhood or in our youth that regrets for a lost paradise follow us throughout our adult lives. Such regrets, as the biography of another poet shows, may acquire a dangerous strength. Had Charles Baudelaire's childhood been less idyllic, once the idyll was brutally destroyed by his mother's remarriage he might have escaped many of the miseries and material humiliations that overcast his later years. François Baudelaire, a cultivated survivor of pre-revolutionary France, a great deal older than his young, elegant, attractive wife, had died when their only child was six; and from February 1827 until November 1828 Charles and his mother had inhabited an emotional heaven-on-earth, the 'green paradise of childish loves', to which his imagination constantly returned. Every detail of their life together was precious – Madame Baudelaire's little house near Paris, '*nôtre blanche maison, petite mais tranquille*', with its thin suburban shrubbery that enclosed two plaster statues; their devoted maid-servant Mariette, '*la servante au grand coeur*'; and the 'long and silent' meals he and his mother had shared, while a flood of evening sunshine poured across their table.

Baudelaire had loved his mother as her child, but also, he remembered, as a 'precocious dandy', in whom her feminine appeal, even the scent of her furs, kindled his senses and aroused his taste for elegance. But Madame Baudelaire, though devoted to her son, was still young, and needed, if not love, at least masculine protection; and after less than two years of widowhood she accepted the hand of a dashing and distinguished soldier, Lieutenant-Colonel Aupick, later General and French Ambassador to the Sublime Porte. For her it was a sensible and satisfying match; for her jealous and precocious son, an unrelieved catastrophe. Their green paradise was almost immediately laid waste. His step-father, a well-meaning disciplinarian, found first the difficult, suspicious child, then the ill-behaved boy, lastly the extravagant, self-destructive young man, a problem utterly impossible to solve. Aupick seems not to have been unaware that Charles possessed some genuine gifts, and later proposed to secure him a safe position in the diplomatic service, an offer he vehemently refused. Between the two rivals for Madame Aupick's love a lasting peace was never made; and, during a Parisian insurrection, several years after Baudelaire had escaped from tutelage and begun to lead an independent life, a friend encountered him outside a gunsmith's shop, which the mob had just plundered, carrying a brand-new weapon slung over his shoulder, and heard him announce that shooting General Aupick should be his contribution to the struggle.

Although as a child, he said, he had feared Aupick, and, as an adult, had loathed and despised him, it was on his devoted mother, rather than on the tyrant himself, that he focused his angriest and cruellest feelings. Her he punished by punishing himself; now that they could no longer share happiness, he determined that she should participate at second hand in all his griefs and misadventures. The letters she regularly received from him contain a painful record of his sufferings and disappointments, the anxieties and collapse of his long, ignominious liaison with the half-caste actress Jeanne Duval. Yet he refused to abandon a desperate hope that, since Aupick had left the scene, there was still time for them to resurrect the past – '*Ah! chère mère, est-il encore temps pour que nous serons heureux?*' – despite his age (he was now forty years old), his mountain of debts and, he suspected, the gradual breakdown of his will.

Yet art often defies life by extracting harmony from personal confusion; and, when he was thirty-seven, the poet had already produced his justificatory masterpiece, *Les Fleurs du Mal*, the volume that, according to Marcel Proust, unfolds the spacious 'landscape of his genius', where each poem is only a fragment of the whole, but, once we have read it, links up, as part of a magnificent general scheme, with the poems it follows or precedes. Baudelaire's fellow poets had warmly welcomed his book. Unluckily – Baudelaire was always an unlucky man – at the same time it attracted the attention of the Napoleonic police; and both writer and publisher were prosecuted, and found guilty of an offence against moral and religious standards. Certain poems were suppressed; the poet was fined three hundred francs. But a second edition was issued; and in 1861, undeterred by his recent reverses, he made a courageous, though somewhat half-hearted, attempt to join the Immortals at the French Academy, and began a candidate's customary round of visits. Alfred de Vigny was encouraging; Lamartine seemed 'aimable'. An old family friend, however, whom he had expected to support him, proved peculiarly unhelpful.

Baudelaire was attached to Sainte-Beuve, one of his mother's guests, a man considerably older than himself, and even affected to admire his poems; but the distinguished critic, having an instinctively cautious nature, felt that his championship of Madame Aupick's wayward son must not appear too unreserved; and his mention of the poet in the influential column that he published every Monday was disappointingly evasive. The new candidate, he assured his middle-class readers, was by no means the literary werewolf his enemies would have had them think, but a 'polite' and 'deferential' personage, a pleasant, well-spoken young man, despite the fact that his creative habits were odd, and that, in the literary world, he chose to inhabit a 'singular kiosk', where he sat and smoked his hubble-bubble 'on the furthest point of the romantic Kamtchatka'.

Sainte-Beuve's faint praise was so obviously measured out that it did his subject little harm; and his appearance in the present context may require some explanation. Unlike the other writers from whose pronouncements I have quoted, Sainte-Beuve again and again denied that his memories had ever brought him happiness. 'My evil, nay my crime', he wailed, 'is that I

have never been loved as I have wished to be loved. This is the secret of my whole insane existence, a life spent without consistency, without self-discipline, without an aim, without confidence even in the work that remains for me to do'. Later – once more our source is the Goncourts' diary – his confidante was the Emperor's cousin, the generous and warm-hearted Princesse Mathilde. She had no idea, he said, how much it meant to a man, the knowledge that real love had escaped him; which, in his case, was accompanied by a premonition that, now he was so old and ugly, were such a heavenly gift still to come his way, he would no doubt appear ridiculous.

Sainte-Beuve's ugliness has often been described. Short and stout, long-nosed and large-eared, he was said to resemble either a shuffling sacristan or a rather wicked ginger cat. Balzac and Stendhal, of course, both great men whom he frequently abused, were almost equally inelegant; but their personalities had a tremendous backing of unselfconscious energy and romantic zeal that irradiated their awkward looks. Sainte-Beuve's appearance, on the other hand, seems to have reflected something discordant in his private character – a curious streak of spite and envy. 'One of man's most veritable satisfactions', he wrote, 'is when a woman he has passionately desired, and who has obstinately refused to accord him her favours, ceases to be beautiful'. Entirely different was Stendhal's association with his past, which, during his literary life, had taught him so many valuable lessons, and, as an adventurous collector of experiences, he had often thoroughly enjoyed. He had no desire to see its images defaced, and, looking back, still felt a tenderly grateful regard for a woman – indeed, for a succession of women – who had either deserted or rejected him.

2

Rousseau's Enchanted Isle

S AMUEL JOHNSON had so large and powerfully active a mind that he was seldom ashamed to contradict himself; and, although he often declared that human happiness existed only in the future or the past, where imagination and memory alone seemed capable of grasping it, he told Boswell (his reader may recollect) that to be happy was still the wise man's duty. Here he had already had many strong supporters, particularly beyond the Channel. During the classic period of French literature, even the sternly devout Pascal had admitted that all human beings sought happiness, and had implied that, if they set out in pursuit of it, provided their conception of their goal remained sound, and they did not equate happiness with mundane pleasures, they would not necessarily go astray. 'A reasonable mind aspires to happiness', Bossuet announced in one of his sonorous yet mellifluous sermons; while Voltaire, the giant of the next age, attributed our lifelong pursuit to the effect of a natural law that governed our entire existence – an opinion that, in the early twentieth century, André Gide would boldly reaffirm.

It is not the search, but the quality of happiness sought, that has varied from place to place, and year to year; and dramatic political events have sometimes changed its course by inspiring the seeker with new hopes and problems. Such an event was the French Revolution. Men born under the Old Regime, who had lived on into the Napoleonic era, were always aware of the tremendous gulf they had crossed, a chasm that seemed to separate two different worlds. None had made the crossing more safely and adroitly

than Charles-Maurice de Talleyrand-Périgord, arch-turncoat, absentee bishop of Autun, Deputy to the National Assembly in the last years of the Revolution and Minister of Foreign Affairs during the Directory, Consulate and Empire, an office that, after the fall of Napoleon and the restoration of the Bourbons, he almost immediately resumed. Having profited by these diverse experiences, he took a philosophic view of history; and, remembering the vanished world in which he had been brought up, he invented his famous phrase '*la douceur de vivre*' to describe the easy charm of the existence he and his privileged contemporaries had shared.

They, at least, he thought had mastered the art of living – an art that Talleyrand, in his own career, combined with an extraordinary talent for surviving. But he saw the defects of the old world as clearly as he saw its virtues; and his posthumously published memoirs* illustrate both the triumphs of his adult life and the hardships of his childhood. Parental care had not yet come into fashion; '*la mode de soins paternels n'était pas encore arrivée*'; and Talleyrand's parents, who each held a courtly position and could seldom leave Versailles, quickly handed him over to a nurse, at whose cottage near Paris he spent several lonely years. His nurse was a stupid woman; and the boy's fall from a chest-of-drawers on which she had carelessly deposited him left him a demi-cripple for the remainder of his life.

'*Je suis resté boiteux*', he wrote – an humiliating admission for an extremely active man to make. Yet Talleyrand, the cynic and realist, felt no lasting resentment against either his neglectful family or the code of conduct they obeyed. They had their roots in the Périgord; and there, he tells us, 'the manners of the nobility resembled the ancient castles they inhabited'. Little direct light penetrated those solid walls; and such beams as crept through were mercifully subdued. Talleyrand's grandmother, who had retired from the great world and become a rustic Lady Bountiful, had been the first member of his family, indeed almost the first human being, to show him any real love. She was a good Christian of the old school; and he recollected how she would sit ministering to sick peasants in a huge room

* *Mémoires du Prince de Talleyrand, publiés . . . par le Duc de Broglie*, 1891.

nicknamed 'the Apothecary's Shop', which was filled with unguents and medicines compounded at home from traditional prescriptions, bottles of syrups and elixirs, and rolls of linen bandages. Madame de Chalais presided, occupying a velvet arm-chair behind an old black lacquer table, wearing a silk- and ribbon- trimmed dress that suited the time of year, a fur stole, a bonnet and a black cap; while a poor relation held the red velvet, gold-braided bag that contained her missal and one or two works of devotion.

During his early days, glimpses of a harmonious domestic life, Talleyrand added, had been comparatively rare; and later, he said, he had been, he supposed, the only young man of his kind – *'d'une naissance distinguée et appartenant à une famille nombreuse et estimée'* – who never for a whole week had had the consolation of finding himself under his paternal roof. Yet, when he was at last permitted to meet his mother, ageing now but still a fashionable woman of the world, she immediately delighted him. In the portrait he drew, he sums up many of the fine qualities that, as ingredients of *la douceur de vivre*, he remembered and regretted. Her conversation had had a charm, an ease, a lightness he had encountered nowhere else:

> 'She was altogether without pedantic pretensions. She spoke in nuances alone; a *bon mot* never crossed her lips; that would have been far too conspicuous. *Bons mots* are repeated; she wished merely to please, and that what she had said should be then forgotten. A rich stock of phrases, fresh and always delicately appropriate, sufficed to convey the varying turns of her wit'

Both in the French and, at the time, in the English social world, an ability to please, and thus make life more agreeable for one's friends, was accounted a conspicuous virtue. But the well-bred talker shunned excess; 'nothing too much' was still a maxim that 'polite society' respected, and 'enthusiasm' a somewhat terrifying word. If Madame Geoffrin, the rich, dignified middle-class hostess, who entertained French *philosophes* and free-thinkers, as well as Gibbon, Horace Walpole and John Wilkes, thought that the flow of conversation around her table threatened to become violent, she would at once check it by remarking '*Voilà qui est bien*',

which quietly hinted 'We've had enough of that!', and re-direct it into safer channels. A regard for *bienséance*, propriety, decorum, fitness, which did not preclude delightful strokes of humour, was evidently one of the characteristics Talleyrand had enjoyed, listening to his parents' conversation; and her example would later disgust him with the loud, dogmatic dialogues he so often heard in Parisian drawing-rooms when the century drew towards its close.

During the reign of Louis XV, he observes, though certain writers and intellectuals – Fontenelle, Montesquieu, Buffon, Voltaire – had already infiltrated aristocratic society, they still respected and, no doubt, admired the manners of the previous epoch, and emulated its careful blend of liberty and licence. But under Louis XVI a roar of talk had arisen, invariably critical and frequently subversive, which sometimes resounded even through Versailles. Social and personal distinctions soon vanished; every barrier went down. The oddest links were formed. The poet Delille, learned translator of Virgil and Milton, dined at Madame de Polignac's house to meet the Queen; the savage aphorist Chamfort, who, after 1789, would coin the revolutionary motto, 'War against the castles; Peace to the cottages!', was observed walking arm-in-arm with a well-known Royalist admiral, the comte de Vaudreuil. Other intellectuals were invited to stay at Marly, the King's country retreat, or supped at the Palace with Madame de Lamballe, Marie-Antoinette's beloved friend. In drawing-rooms and ballrooms, every move the ministers made, and almost every action attributed to the sovereigns, were discussed and usually derided. The young felt particularly sure that, given the opportunity, which would soon come, they were fully capable of governing.

While the Old Regime talked itself to death, the moral and intellectual climate of France underwent a rapid change. 'Sentiments', Talleyrand writes, 'were replaced by philanthropic ideas, passions by the analysis of the human heart; the desire to please by strong opinions; amusements by new plans and projects . . .' These climatic changes, however, although the approach of the Revolution gave them a more definite form, had already begun to appear a good deal earlier in the century. The affection for children, that Talleyrand's parents had lacked, soon became distinctly fashionable; and much-admired artists, notably Greuze and a younger and

Moreau le Jeune's fashionable heroine receives a secret love-letter.

livelier artist, Moreau le Jeune, born in 1741, depicted the beauties of childhood and innocence, and the pleasures of a simple life.

During the seventeenth century La Bruyère had described the French peasants he saw beside the roads as 'certain wild animals, male and female . . . black, livid and burned by the sun . . . chained, as it were, to the land they are always digging and turning over with an unconquerable stubbornness'. But, he remarks indignantly, they, too, 'have a sort of articulate voice, and when they stand up, they exhibit human features'; one must admit that 'they are men'. It was these little-known beings Greuze had humanised in a series of pictures, some of them commissioned by a Russian grand-duke – 'The Father's Curse', 'The Father's Blessing', 'The Punished Son', 'The Village Betrothed' and others, that illustrate the joys and sorrows, the conflicts and reconciliations, of their harsh, laborious lives. Even Moreau le Jeune, whose most attractive plates are scenes of aristocratic life which show how a privileged young woman spent her pleasant, idle days, was prepared at times to change his subject. His heroine, though she is fond of her children, and at breakfast gives them, as a special treat, a lump of sugar soaked in coffee, is clearly a light-minded worldling; and, when she and her legitimate consort attend the opera, she allows a secret note to be slipped into her hand. But among Moreau le Jeune's charming glimpses of high life we also find a plate he called *Le Vrai Bonheur*, the background of true happiness being a modest rustic cottage, where a sturdy labourer, who has just returned from his work, arrives home to be greeted by his ancient mother, his wife, his handsome, well-grown babes and their amiable shaggy dog.

'*Le Vrai Bonheur*', drawn by Moreau le Jeune but engraved by a different artist, Simonet, was first published in 1776; and, a year later, Jean-Jacques Rousseau, who would die in 1778, was writing the fifth of his *Rêveries du Promeneur Solitaire*, the autobiographical essay that described the climax of his long musings on the theme of human happiness, by which he meant primarily his own happiness; for every line of investigation that Rousseau pursued soon led back towards himself. In his vocabulary, *bonheur* was a key-word; few writers have employed it more often; it represented the ultimate objective of all his dreams and hopes; and, having found and lost it during his own youth, as he grew older he turned his attention to the problems of the world at large, and, much more effectively than any

'True Happiness'; the labourer's home-coming.

drawing-room theorist, would help to undermine the foundations of the established social system.

Born in 1712, the son of a prosperous Genevan watchmaker, Jean-Jacques Rousseau had a naturally impatient and demanding spirit, and enjoyed his first great adult experience at the age of fifteen, when, having decided to become a Catholic, he left his father's house and, at Annecy, encountered Madame de Warens, a well-known patroness of deserving Catholic converts, whom he had expected to find a plain good-doing dowager, but who proved to be a voluptuous twenty-nine-year-old woman, 'radiant with charm', her 'blue eyes filled with sweetness', and who had soon amicably seduced him. His attachment to Madame de Warens, henceforward his adored '*Maman*', protectress, counsellor and bedfellow, provided by far the calmest and happiest chapter of an otherwise distressful life. He was already a vagrant; but not until he and Madame de Warens had parted did his adult wander-years begin – the years when he became a haunted fugitive, constantly in flight, though he had rich and powerful admirers, from real or half-imaginary foes. It is hard to avoid the suspicion that he secretly welcomed his numerous and often humiliating reverses – he had been, his autobiography tells us, a masochist and exhibitionist since childhood – and that failure appealed to him more than any stroke of good fortune.

Even at Court he had once enjoyed a triumph. Among his many gifts were his understanding of music and his skill as a composer;* and in 1752 his pastoral operetta, *Le Devin du Village*,† so delighted Madame de Pompadour and Louis XV, that its first performance at the Palace of Fontainebleau was magnificently successful. Fame and security now seemed close indeed; but Rousseau, learning that next day he was to be presented to the King, who would utter a few words of congratulation, and that he himself must prepare a ceremonious speech, remembered that he had a physical infirmity which sometimes bound him to his chamber-pot, took fright and quickly left the Palace – behaviour that much

---

* Rousseau was a keen admirer of Gluck, for whom he worked as a copyist, until he came to suspect that the great composer was somehow taking sides against him.
† It has been occasionally revived; but, according to Martin Cooper, author of *Gluck*, 1935, it is 'set . . . in a musical idiom simple to the verge of childishness', and may have owed its success to the fact that it persuaded the French world that there was 'still hope for French music.'

displeased the sovereign, who talked of having him arrested and thrown into gaol.

Two years later, Latour painted his portrait; and Diderot, as professional art-critic, found it an absurdly misleading likeness. Rousseau was already a professional writer, author of a *Discourse on the Sciences and the Arts*, where he had attacked contemporary *philosophes* and the whole principle of eighteenth-century Enlightenment; and what Diderot had hoped for, he said, was a work that immortalised 'the Censor of our literature, the Cato, the Brutus of our age'; whereas Latour seemed to have gone out of his way to depict a very different man – 'the composer of *Le Devin du Village*, well-dressed, well-powdered, and ridiculously seated in a cane chair'. When Diderot published his criticism, however, Rousseau had already changed his mask; his likeness to a respectable, even slightly fashionable, citizen was a *persona* that he very soon abandoned. He wished to be regarded as a quiet, hard-working craftsman, no longer the successful composer but a laborious copyist of music, who knew how to 'live in poverty' and hoped, at last, to 'die in independence'.

That was the part he now assumed and, until the end, would resolutely play. Rousseau's 'awareness of living an exemplary life never left him', writes a recent French biographer.* He prized his own virtue above all else. Yet that virtue, as he did not hesitate to admit in his *Confessions*, which he began to read aloud during the last decade of his existence, had a decidedly unstable basis. His detractors presently discovered, and he himself would latterly tell the world, that he and his humble mistress, Thérèse Le Vasseur, had consigned their five bastard infants to the grim Parisian Foundling Hospital, whence it was unlikely they would re-emerge; and this horrid story, which the ever-attentive Voltaire very soon picked up, haunted him throughout his closing years. Madame d'Épinay's assertion that he was 'a moral dwarf on stilts' may reflect the malice of an aggrieved and disappointed friend; but there seems no doubt that his virtues and his vices, his fierce sincerity and his touches of sly humbug, were curiously intermixed, and that the legend of Rousseau the modern Cato or Brutus needs a good deal of critical revision.

* Jean Guéhenno: *Jean-Jacques Rousseau*, 1962.

Jean-Jacques Rousseau, after Latour's portrait; his 'aware-ness of leading an exemplary life never left him.'

During his lifetime, though often disputed both by enemies and by friends turned foe, it was still enthusiastically accepted – for example, by James Boswell, then on the Grand Tour, who, preparatory to visiting Rousseau at Môtiers, his secluded Swiss retreat, 'swore solemnly' that, meanwhile, he would neither 'talk as an infidel' nor 'enjoy a woman . . .' The momentous interview that followed, between the young Scottish laird and his 'Dear and Singular Philosopher', took place early in December 1764. Having been welcomed by the forty-three-year-old Mademoiselle Le Vasseur – the romantic tourist, strangely enough, calls her 'a little, lively, neat French girl' – and conducted up a 'darkish stair' and into a room that served as vestibule and kitchen, Boswell, dressed for the occasion in a 'scarlet and gold-laced coat' and 'a great coat of Green Camlet lined with Foxskin Fur', and carrying under his arm 'a hat with sollid gold lace, at least with the air of being sollid', confronted 'a genteel black man in the dress of an Armenian'. Altogether Boswell paid the famous 'Solitary' no less than five prolonged visits; and they found many subjects to discuss – perverse theologians whom the sage ridiculed; Rousseau's health; Boswell's character and aims; his desire to set up a harem of thirty peasant virgins he would impregnate and finally marry off, a suggestion that Rousseau mildly deprecated, though polygamy, he agreed, was a practice of which he did not altogether disapprove; and, yet more important, whether the great man believed that he was still a Christian. 'Each stood steady and watched the other's looks. He struck his breast and replied, *"Oui – je me pique de l'être"* ' – a slightly ambiguous phrase, which might perhaps be translated: 'Yes – I like to think I am'.

On this third visit, besides investigating Rousseau's religious convictions, the searcher for truth made a particularly bold request: 'Will you, Sir, assume direction of me?' he asked. 'I cannot. I can be responsible only for myself', Rousseau answered, adding 'I am in pain. I need a chamber-pot every minute'. Though the sage often spoke of his illness and tiredness, and sometimes begged the young man to cut his visits short, Boswell cheerfully persisted; and the record he kept at the time shows the extraordinary influence Rousseau exercised, despite his own very obvious failings, upon the thoughts and conduct of his fellow men. A wanderer himself, always unsure of his way, he became their special guide. Boswell's strongest and steadiest mentor, of course, indignantly rejected him. He thought Rousseau, Johnson told Boswell, 'one of the worst of men; a

rascal who ought to be hunted out of society . . . I would sooner sign a sentence for his transportation, than that of any felon who has gone from the Old Bailey these many years'. Boswell, determined that such an exciting controversy should not subside, then boldly brought in Voltaire's name: 'Sir, do you think him as bad a man as Voltaire?' 'Why, Sir,' Johnson responded, 'it is difficult to settle the proportion of iniquity between them'.

Both in principle and in their private attitude towards mankind Johnson and Rousseau were irreconcilable opponents. Johnson had a voracious appetite for life, and was passionately concerned with the welfare of individual men and women; while Rousseau, although he was persuaded that he loved the human race, or would have loved it if he could, followed a solitary, self-centred course and, among a host of associates, protectors, disciples, made comparatively few friends whose opinions and support he valued. Here one remembers another literary dispute, held some hundred-and-fifty years later, when Henry James, writing to the youthful H.G. Wells, described their fundamental difference. 'You', he explained, 'don't care for humanity but think they are to be improved. I love humanity but know they are not!' Johnson, too, despite his capacity for deep affection, was a life-long pessimist; Rousseau, the suspicious and resentful exile, was an inveterate reformer, and launched the doctrine of 'human perfectibility' that made so strong, and often so confusing, an appeal to English nineteenth-century Romantic poets. He was a teacher; but his chief aim was primarily to teach himself; if he desired to learn, he confessed, it was primarily in order to understand his own character.

Happiness was also a subject on which Rousseau and Johnson inevitably disagreed. For Johnson, a transitory boon; for Rousseau, it was a natural human right. Though he always looked back on the years he had spent with Madame de Warens as his 'land of lost content' – he would have liked, he said, to erect a golden railing around the place where they had first met* – and, two years before he encountered Boswell, declared that his whole adult life had been a mere tissue of 'trouble, anguish and pain', he had never abandoned the pursuit of happiness, and at length, in 1765, when his sufferings seem to have grown most acute, on a little island amid the Swiss

* Such a railing was erected in the nineteenth century, but unfortunately somewhat misplaced.

mountains he felt that he had definitely reached his goal. He did not begin to describe his memorable achievement, however, until some eleven years had passed; and by then he had retired to Paris, where his last disciple, Bernardin de Saint-Pierre, future author of that strange tropical romance *Paul et Virginie*, who at the moment was planning to depict 'a society that owed its happiness only to the laws of nature and virtue', paid him many long visits.

In 1772, Rousseau's rooms above the Rue Plâtrière certainly suited a philosopher. They were on the fourth floor; and the bedroom, which was also his workroom, contained only two small beds, covered with blue-and-white-striped cotton cloth, a chest-of-drawers, a table and a few chairs. On the walls hung a map of the Forest of Montmorency, where he had once lived, and of which he had happy recollections, and an engraved portrait of King George III, who, during Rousseau's disastrous expedition to England under David Hume's wing, had offered him a pension of £100 a year, and whom, though he had then elaborately refused it, he still regarded as his benefactor. Mademoiselle Le Vasseur, now styled 'Madame Rousseau' after an unorthodox ceremony he had organised, sat near him quietly mending linen; a canary sang in its cage; sparrows picked up crumbs from the window-sills; and Bernardin noticed a multitude of pots and boxes that he had filled with plants and wild flowers. Close to Rousseau — then sixty-four years old, a bright-eyed elderly man, his expression sometimes deeply sad, sometimes gay and sharply animated — stood a spinet, symbol of his musical interests, on which he occasionally tried out an air.

Rousseau changed his lodgings for the last time in the early summer of 1778. The Rue Plâtrière was growing too expensive; and the marquis de Girardin, a keen admirer of *La Nouvelle Héloïse*, proposed to build him a thatched cottage at Ermenonville near Senlis, and meanwhile offered him a small pavilion opposite his own château. There he died on July 4th, 1778, clasping Thérèse's hand, without, she told his disciples, 'uttering a single word';* and it was there he wrote the closing sections of *Les Rêveries du*

---

* Afterwards she frequently changed her story, and informed Moreau le Jeune, who painted a portrait of the dying sage seated at his open window, that he had exclaimed 'Be comforted; you can see how pure and serene the heavens are. Well, I am on my way there'.

Promeneur Solitaire, begun at his Parisian rooms, the extraordinary work in which he both looks back to his early youth, when he was Madame de Warens' pupil, and describes and analyses the moment of supreme happiness beside the Lac de Bienne he had enjoyed twelve years ago. His major works already lay years behind him – *Julie, ou la Nouvelle Héloise*, published in 1761, his romantic epistolary novel, which even Boswell conceded 'might do harm', but immediately became a guide-book to the realms of sensation and emotion carried around by eighteenth-century lovers;* *Emile*, his treatise on educational methods; and *Le Contrat Social*, a study of the proper relationship between the individual and society, which, like *Emile*, had appeared and been officially banned in 1762.

These works had given Rousseau the place he deserved beside his ancient adversary Voltaire, who had long watched him from a cautious distance, as a revolutionary liberator of the European mind. But, during his old age, he was less concerned with the general state of humanity, and how it might shed its chains, than with the problem of his own existence. Happiness was a subject that still absorbed him; and he had come to believe that it could only be achieved through a kind of sublimated self-regard.†
'*Le moi est haïssable*', Pascal had declared; but Rousseau contradicts that gloomy sentence. Far from abandoning and detesting the Self, one must cultivate an exalted self-love. '*Il faut être soi.*' Nature was the ultimate pattern of Virtue; and, as Natural Man does, one must rely for happiness on the simple sense of living.

Twice, he thought, he had definitely achieved happiness; and of the first occasion he was reminded in April 1788, when the sound of bells announcing Palm Sunday reminded him that it was now 'exactly fifty years since I first made the acquaintance of Madame de Warens . . . This first encounter determined the course of my whole life.' Never a day went by, he wrote in his last manuscript, 'but I remember with tender delight that unique and brief space of time when I was able to be myself to the full,

* Among these enthusiasts were Georgiana, Duchess of Devonshire, her beloved friend Lady Elizabeth Foster, and Queen Victoria's father, the Duke of Kent. All three included *La Nouvelle Héloise* in their travelling libraries.
† For an admirable discussion of Rousseau's views, see Marcel Raymond's introduction to *Les Rêveries du Promeneur Solitaire*, 1948.

without adulteration or impediment, and during which I can truly say I lived . . .' The second, a much more transitory experience, is recorded in the *Rêveries*; but it produced no permanently rewarding sequel, and had had a troubled and disturbing prelude.

In 1765 his public persecutors, both French and Swiss, seemed to outnumber his devoted allies; and Rousseau's paranoiac strain, which dramatised evey mishap and detected 'conspiracies' where none existed, became alarmingly apparent. But, now and then, his hardships were real enough. On Swiss soil he had expected freedom and peace; that autumn, however, the rustic inhabitants of Môtiers unexpectedly sided with the enemy. The local pastor, who had once been an admiring acquaintance, but had recently developed, Rousseau thought he noticed, a 'sinister' and 'sombre' look, chose to denounce him from the pulpit. He was insulted as he walked the streets; and, at home, he suffered 'lapidation'; mysterious assailants stoned his lodgings.

From these ugly scenes he sought a new refuge, on the little Ile Saint-Pierre, surrounded by the neighbouring Lac de Bienne, where the custodian of the island's only decent house had good-naturedly agreed to shelter him provided that he gave no trouble. Rousseau, like Shelley, loved water; and he was always especially fond of islands, which he associated with his favourite novel, *The Life and Strange Surprising Adventures of Robinson Crusoe*. Both he and his last friend Bernardin were ardent 'Robinsonians'; and the Ile Saint-Pierre was an almost perfect island of its kind, nearly as well-stocked as the miniature commonwealth Defoe had created for his industrious castaway. Part wild, part carefully cultivated, it contained hills and valleys, fields, vineyards, woodlands, orchards and shady meadows; and Rousseau suggested to his host that, on a much smaller neighbouring island, they should set up a colony of rabbits. The installation of the colony, which would no doubt have prospered and multiplied had its founders recollected that Swiss winters are often very harsh, was celebrated with rustic merriment. 'The pilot of the Argonauts', he wrote, 'could not have been prouder than I was' as he conducted the rabbit-colonists across the water to their new home.

The Ile Saint-Pierre was also a botanical heaven; and botany, since he had acquired a copy of Linnaeus' *Systema naturala*, was now among the

Solitary's strongest passions. Nothing, he recorded, could have given him so much pleasure, such ecstasy indeed, as every discovery he made about the structure and organisation of the vegetable world, and the part played by its generative organs in the fructification of a species. Every detail pleased his eye, and added fresh colour to his vision of a universe beautifully and harmoniously planned. He had always enjoyed walking, if possible walking alone; and the proximity of the Lac de Bienne made his solitary excursions around the island doubly soothing and delightful. Sometimes he would remain on shore; but, if the weather were calm, he would row out towards the centre of the lake and, his gaze turned to the sky, let his boat drift calmly and aimlessly along, directed by some gentle current.

Thus, during this brief holiday, from September to October 1765, passed on or near the Lac de Bienne, Rousseau achieved his second experience of almost undiluted happiness; and, whereas the first had originated in a moving personal relationship, the second was a solitary rapture. When he opened the *Première Promenade*, his spirits were still at the lowest level; and he had subsided yet again into paranoiac self-pity. 'So here I am,' he announced, 'alone on the earth, now lacking brother, neighbour, friend, or any company except my own. The most sociable and the most affectionate of men has been unanimously proscribed. In the refinement of their hatred, they have sought to discover the torture that my sensitive soul would find most cruel; and they have violently broken the links that attached me to them. I should have loved my fellow men despite themselves.'

Then gradually, from the sorrows of his present position that recalled an evil dream, his memory shifted back to his beloved island, on which, many years earlier, he had enjoyed a momentary peace. Above all else, it had been the sound of the waters that had relieved his inward misery. As the evening approached, he would walk down towards the lake; and there the rhythmic flux and reflux of wavelets that constantly broke against the shore would chase away his agitation and, without obliging him to think, make him vividly and delightfully aware of his own separate existence. Wild pleasures and keen affections, he had already often noticed, were those he remembered least distinctly. Far more durable were the rare moments when the soul discovered a firm enough resting-place – '*une assiette assez solide*' – to give it the support that it demanded; when Past and Future

appeared equally unreal; when the idea of Time completely lost its power; and one enjoyed a complete and perfect happiness – '*un bonheur, parfait et plein*' – that left no inward need unsatisfied. So long as this state of mind endured, '*on se suffit à soi-même comme Dieu*' – the happy man, like his Creator, was sufficient to himself.

Rousseau's discovery of true happiness as an ecstatic recognition and realisation of the Self marks the point at which, he says, 'I bade goodbye to my century and my contemporaries', and, we now see, had begun to fore-shadow the Romantic Movement. Earlier, having taught his fellow men that they must love and reverence Nature, and especially adore the Alps, he had explained that he could never have spent so many days 'regarding these magnificent landscapes, had I not found still greater pleasure in the conversation of the inhabitants'. But, since he had turned his back on an unkind world, which, he felt, had finally rejected him, untroubled solitude was all that he asked from life. Real happiness was only to be found within the magic circle of the ego.

3

```
┌──────────────────────────┐
│  'A New Idea in Europe'   │
└──────────────────────────┘
```

Rousseau had said that not until some revolution transformed society would mankind be prepared to do him justice; and, in fact, when just eleven years and ten days after his death at Ermenonville, the expected storm broke, although, since Diderot had styled him the Cato or Brutus of the age he had never wanted admirers, it immediately enlarged his fame; he was canonised as a revolutionary saint; and his busts and portraits were sold throughout France, or employed to decorate every kind of domestic object from snuffboxes to pieces of household crockery.* He had been well aware, however, that violent social changes, if they occurred might perhaps prove cruel and destructive; for there was always a danger, he prophesied, that new laws, under the malign influence of human passions, might be used to serve the old nefarious ends; and certainly the French Revolution, in its blood-thirsty later period, would have astonished and appalled him.

Yet, during the first savage years of the Republic, two of his disciples led the way, and preached and organised the Terror – a ferocious bureaucrat, Maximilien Robespierre, who shared the prophet's cult of 'sensibility', and an impassioned orator, Robespierre's devoted lieutenant Saint-Just, whose contribution to the study of happiness is among the strangest yet made, so little does it accord with what we know of his character or of his

---

* Jean Guéhenno, op. cit. Napoleon himself had a walking-stick with Rousseau's portrait embedded in the handle.

[41]

own extraordinary life. Once their savage regime had suddenly collapsed, they would die both on the same day – July 28th, 1794 – and on the same scaffold. Antoine Louis Léon de Richebourg de Saint-Just was then twenty-six, a tall, dark-haired young man, *'d'une belle et imposante physiognomie'*, austere, calm, dignified, elegantly dressed. Despite his patrician air and lofty-sounding name, his origins were fairly modest. The only son of an old soldier, with his two sisters he had been brought up by their widowed mother at a Picard country-town called Blérancourt; and there, during his early manhood, almost for the last time, Saint-Just seems to have exhibited some of the usual human weaknesses. Thus, when he was nineteen, his mother accused him of having stolen and carried off to Paris certain valuable pieces of family plate, a pair of gold-mounted pistols and a precious ring, and had had him temporarily imprisoned; while, about the same period, he was said also to have run away with a youthful married woman. The story remains obscure; but he wrote some romantic verses, in which he told his readers that life was a dream,* advised them to close their eyes and, eyelids lowered, cull its transitory joys, and declared that, at least in imagination, he himself was now 'a King on Earth', punishing the wicked and rewarding virtue.

No sooner, during July 1789, had news of the Revolution reached Blérancourt than such adolescent velleities were forever left behind. He plunged into local politics, spoke at republican clubs, where his orations were greatly admired, and enlisted as an officer of the republican National Guard. Saint-Just would always impress his contemporaries not only by his compulsive eloquence but by the dramatic poses he assumed. In 1790, for example, while he was still at Blérancourt, he conducted a deputation of peasants to the château of a local nobleman; and, hearing that the Count had gone out, he employed the stick he held to decapitate a tall flowering plant underneath the grandee's windows, then, having executed that sternly significant gesture, turned and led his fellow patriots away.

Meanwhile, besides carrying a petition on behalf of the citizens of Blérancourt to the National Assembly, he addressed an eulogistic letter to his hero Robespierre – 'I do not know you', he wrote, 'but you are a great

* *'Tout nous le dit: Oui, la vie est un songe. Les yeux fermés, rêvons tranquillement . . .'*

man'; and, at an early meeting, that 'Messiah of the People' quickly recognised the bold young stranger as his predestined John the Baptist. Saint-Just was already well aware of what the situation offered him – the means of rising to the surface of his age; '*je me sens* (he declared) *de quoi surnager dans le siècle*'. His new allies included Camille Desmoulins, an unsuccessful barrister but a naturally accomplished demagogue, whose wild impromptu harangue, delivered on July 11th 1789, from a café table-top to the Sunday crowd that filled the Palais Royal's gardens, had sent his fellow patriots pouring out through the streets and, two days later, once they had gathered arms, inspired the siege and capture of the Bastille.

Supported by Robespierre and Desmoulins, Saint-Just began to establish his position; but Desmoulins, as he watched his protégé's rise, eventually became a critic. He had noticed Saint-Just's arrogance and look of indomitable self-esteem. 'One sees', he wrote, 'both from his carriage and from his attitude, that he regards his head as the corner-stone of the Republic, and that he carries it on his shoulders with respect, like a holy sacrament'; to which Saint-Just replied that, if Desmoulins were not careful, he might presently have to carry his own head under his arm in the style of the legendary St. Denis. It was a prophetic retort; at the end of March 1794, less than five months before his death, and fifteen months after the execution of the King (which he had strongly advocated), Saint-Just headed the prosecution of nine previous colleagues, among them Desmoulins and the mighty Danton, and seven of their younger assistants, and framed an eloquent speech demanding the death-penalty. When he wrote his memoirs, the future Director, the odious opportunist Paul Barras, described the young prosecutor's solemn approach to the tribune, and, as he spoke, the incisive downward gesture of his right hand, with which he repeatedly cut the air, and seemed horribly to imitate the guillotine's descending blade.

Desmoulins, though his early revolutionary record was savage enough, and he had adopted the ferocious nickname '*Procureur Général de la Lanterne*', or '*Minister of the Street-lamp*' – the usual gibbet of aristocrats and suspected Royalists – had recently suggested that a 'committee of mercy' should be set up. But both Saint-Just and Robespierre prided themselves on their conscientious lack of pity. Terrorism, they had

decided, must remain the order of the day; their avowed intention was to keep it busily at work – '*maintenir partout à l'ordre du jour la terreur*'; and they continued to anticipate, admittedly on a far less extensive scale, the hideous achievements of twentieth-century dictators, until, during the explosive 'days of Thermidor', July 1794, Robespierre was received in the rebellious Convention with loud cries of '*A bas le tyran!*'

The two arch-terrorists, however, had had some redeeming human traits. No one could question the younger man's courage or loyalty. When Robespierre was shouted down, Saint-Just, obliged to desert the tribune and occupy a slightly lower place, still confronted the vociferous opposition in his customary defiant pose, '*immobile, impassible, inébranlable*'; and, when he mounted the scaffold, where Robespierre lay helpless and speechless, a bloody bandage wrapped around a shattered jaw, Saint-Just awaited death '*avec le calme stoïque et l'impassibilité froide*' that he had already displayed facing German guns on an official expedition to the battle-front. Robespierre was the more prosaic character; he had many of the attributes, some of the good qualities even, of a conscientious civil servant. Nor did he entirely lack feeling; with his exigent cult of republican 'virtue', to which every other consideration must be sacrificed, he combined the personal idealism that he had learned from Rousseau. Like Jean-Jacques he lived quietly and simply; and Barras remembered how he and a fellow politician had visited him at his small, uncomfortable Parisian rooms. His barber had just attended him; as always, Robespierre was carefully arrayed. 'But a film of powder masked his pallid face; and amid the powder one saw a pair of eyes, whose dimness the heavy spectacles he wore usually concealed in public'. He now turned them on Barras, staring fixedly and silently; and, throughout the entire interview, while Barras's colleague made him a lengthy speech, describing their ungrateful treatment by the National Convention, he uttered not a single word.

On the eve of their death, although they were determined that the Terror must continue, Robespierre and Saint-Just were meditating a minor domestic reform, designed to civilise the Revolution and smooth the roughness of proletarian manners. They set their *sanculotte* followers a good example – Robespierre with his expensively dressed hair; Saint-Just with his ear-rings and his high stock. The moment had come, they

believed, when the people must begin to enjoy their triumphs; '*la révolution*', said Saint-Just, '*est l'ouvrage du peuple; il est temps qu'il en jouisse*'. Enjoyment need no longer be exiled from the revolutionary world, provided, of course, that it was allied to virtue, and never besmirched by aristocratic excesses. He now offered the liberated French people a modest share of human pleasures – 'the satisfaction of detesting tyranny', and 'of inhabiting a humble cottage, beside a fertile field that your own hands have tilled'. Such, he thought, was the spirit of the modern age. On the *8 Ventôse l'an II* (otherwise February 26th 1794), when he delivered a report to the Convention, 'Happiness', he announced, 'is a new idea in Europe.'

To the question that Saint-Just's strange statement must immediately provoke – why the arch terrorist, having once recognised the value of happiness, should then have asserted that among his own countrymen it was a completely new idea – we can find, no doubt, a simple answer: the idea's birthplace, he evidently assumed, had been far away across the Atlantic Ocean, where in 1776 the valiant young American Colonists had proclaimed their independence. Since that day America had replaced England as the modern Promised Land. When Voltaire, during the early summer of 1726, having just emerged from the Bastille, first set foot on British soil, nearly everything he saw and heard delighted him – the grace of English equestriennes managing their spirited horses, the prosperity and dignity of London merchants, the homage writers and scientists received, and the liberal opinions that great noblemen and members of the government themselves were not afraid to voice. Thus he had begun his revolutionary career; he now felt that his mission was to combat all the prejudices and superstitions that victimised his own country; and, after his return, he published a French edition of the book he entitled *Lettres philosophiques*, in which, though he abused England's greatest poet – Shakespeare puzzled and revolted him* – he applauded the whole English social system; with the result that his rooms were searched, his private papers seized, and the book was condemned to be burned by the public executioner.

As the century went on and political unrest grew, what particularly roused the impatience of the middle and upper classes, wrote a French

---

* '*C'est une pièce grossière et barbare*', he wrote of *Hamlet*, '*qui ne serait pas supportée par la plus vile populace de la France et d'Italie*'.

nobleman, the comte de Ségur, was the contrast between their present situation and that of their immediate neighbours. Visiting Englishmen enjoyed an unprecedented popularity. The 1760s were the age of Anglomania, when, recorded Edward Gibbon, 'our opinions, our fashions, even our games, were adopted in France . . . and every Englishman was supposed to be born a patriot and a philosopher'. English writers received a particularly warm welcome; and their works were read and discussed in Paris almost as soon as they appeared.

A special hero, both of fashionable society and of the French intelligentsia, was David Hume, private secretary to the British Ambassador since 1763, whose massive *History of England* – his great enquiry into the nature of the Human Understanding was still comparatively little known – had gained him innumerable French admirers. He never outlived his welcome. Until, at last, he reluctantly left Paris, he had eaten 'nothing but Ambrosia', he said, drunk 'nothing but Nectar', breathed 'nothing but Incense', and trodden on 'nothing but Flowers'. Such were the rewards of enlightenment. The Scottish historian was a man who appreciated pleasure and had always aimed at happiness. Yet, despite his middle-aged contentment, Hume was a reformed depressive. His youth had been overcast by the type of deep melancholy that his contemporaries labelled 'hypochondria'; from which he had only escaped by recognising its physical origins and taking strenuous counter-measures that included regular exercise, 'Anti-hysteric Pills' and a pint of claret every day.

Unlike Boswell, he had gradually conquered his affliction; and it was his air of cheerfulness and unselfconscious equanimity that most delighted his Parisian friends, among them the fascinating Madame de Boufflers (nicknamed 'Madam Blewflower' by the crowd on her visit to London, during which she paid Samuel Johnson a rapid visit) with whom he very nearly fell in love. Hume's vogue at a time, Madame d'Épinay relates, when, thanks to his personal charm and his literary reputation, 'all the prettiest women were devoted to him and he attended all the smartest supper-parties', lasted from 1763 to January 1766. But the French are a volatile race; and ten years later they responded just as readily to a second foreign hero. The septuagenarian Benjamin Franklin, intermediary between France and the New World, had arrived upon a crucial diplomatic mission.

His task was to organise the shipment of arms and supplies to the embattled Colonists; and before he sailed, he had worked with the committee that produced the Declaration of Independence, signed on August 2nd, 1776.* Never has the joint production of a committee, which took its basic material from a number of different sources, had a more tremendous effect or been more eloquently, yet more simply and more directly, worded. Its object, long afterwards declared Thomas Jefferson, one of its chief authors, 'was not to find out new principles, or new arguments . . . but to place before mankind the common sense of the subject, in terms so plain and firm as to command their assent . . . It was intended to be an expression of the American mind . . . All its authority rests . . . on the harmonizing sentiments of the day.'

Hence the famous lines that soon resounded through France:

'We hold these truths to be self-evident: that all men are created equal; that they were endowed by their Creator with certain inalienable rights; that among these are life, liberty, and the pursuit of happiness'.

Both the constitutions of the new Thirteen States and the Declaration itself were quickly translated into French by the high-minded young duc de la Rochefoucauld, whose mother, Franklin's close friend, would, in 1792, watch him being stoned to death by a revolutionary mob; and the Declaration caused so much excitement that the authorities hastened to suppress it. Yet Franklin escaped reproof; and, after some fifteen months' delay, caused by the protests of the British Ambassador, he was graciously received at Versailles. The costume he assumed on this momentous occasion – a russet velvet coat and white stockings: his hair loose and his spectacles on his nose, a white hat (which the aged Madame du Deffand, writing to Horace Walpole, conjectured might be a symbol of liberty) carried underneath his arm – suggested a diplomatic combination of European correctitude and American *sans gêne*. Louis XVI's response was no less diplomatic. He had been praying in his chapel; his hair was undressed; no preparations, it seemed, had been made to receive the

* Independence was neither declared on July 4th (as popular historians have assumed) nor was the Declaration fully signed until August 2nd. See James Truslow Adams: *The Living Jefferson*, 1936.

David Hume; print after a portrait by Allan Ramsay, which shows his resemblance to a 'turtle-eating English alderman'.

envoys. But, as soon as they were introduced, the King assumed 'a noble posture'. He spoke first, 'with more care and graciousness', remembered a veteran courtier, than he had ever heard the sovereign display before. 'He said: "Firmly assure Congress of my friendship . . ." M. Franklin, very nobly, thanked him in the name of America, and said: "Your Majesty may count on the gratitude of Congress and its faithful observance of the pledges it now takes." '*

By this time, Franklin had become the cynosure of Parisian society, though his physical appearance, like that of the 'plump and large and rosy' Hume, said by critics to have resembled a 'turtle-eating' London alderman, was not immediately attractive. Yet he, too, had uncommon personal charm; and his benevolently wrinkled face, bald cranium and thin, grey, unpowdered locks, certainly increased his fascination. Before long a series of brilliant French ladies addressed him as their '*cher Papa*'. These devotees included Madame d'Houdetot, formerly Rousseau's beloved; the beautiful Madame Brillon, who occasionally sat on Papa's knee, though she allowed him 'only some kisses'; and Madame Helvétius, widow of the distinguished *philosophe*, to whom he once proposed marriage.

Franklin, even during his last years, was always much concerned with love; and, if many of his Parisian love-affairs remained platonic, that was evidently against his will. But, whether he succeeded or failed, seen through the eyes of his French admirers his liaisons did him no discredit. Indeed, they enhanced his reputation as a blend of sage and *homme du monde* – a man, moreover, who displayed extraordinary skill in the conduct of his own existence. His 'most original trait', decided an early nineteenth-century enthusiast, was 'his art of living in the best fashion for himself and for others, making the most effective use of all the tools nature has placed at the disposal of man . . . He would eat, sleep, work whenever he saw fit . . . so that there never was a more leisurely man, though he certainly handled a tremendous amount of business.'†

Franklin's ability to combine leisure and business, and the realistic management of life with its imaginative enjoyment, clearly distinguished

---

* The duc de Croy: *Journal inédit*; quoted by Claude-Anne Lopez: *Mon Cher Papa*, 1966.
† Pierre J-G. Cabanis, quoted by Claude-Anne Lopez, op. cit.

him from most of his contemporaries, either in America or in France. He understood and appreciated '*la douceur de vivre*'; yet he was at the same time sternly practical. Anything he did, he did thoroughly; and, during his American youth, when he had gained his livelihood as bookseller, newspaper-publisher, printer and stationer, he also sold across the counter of his shop iron stoves and cakes of soap, Dutch quills and Aleppo ink, Rhode Island cheese, goose feathers, tea, coffee, Bibles, account books and parchment sheets for legal use. As a modern publisher, he was remarkably adventurous; and among the products of his printing-press were the earliest American medical treatise and the first novel, printed at home, that the Colonists had yet seen – Samuel Richardson's *Pamela*, which he brought out in 1794. It was Franklin's inventive genius, however, that had earned him European fame. Once he discovered that lightning was not a divine visitation but a simple form of electricity, he produced a lightning-conductor so neat and effective that it sent a shock of amazement through the scientific world.

Another characteristic Franklin and Jefferson shared, and that made them well-qualified emissaries of the New World, was their deeply-rooted affection for Europe. True, Jefferson had a puritanical strain, and was sometimes shocked by the artificiality and insincerity that he thought he detected in Parisian life; but he considered the French an exceptionally gifted people; and 'were I to proceed to tell you', he assured a friend at home, 'how much I enjoy their architecture, sculpture, painting, music, I should want words.' It was he who commissioned Jean-Antoine Houdon to execute a famous bust of Washington; and he delighted in the remains of Roman architecture he saw on his travels around Southern France. At the *Maison Carrée*, Nismes' almost perfectly preserved Roman temple, he had gazed 'like a lover at his mistress'; while Orange's splendid arch and the 'sublime antiquity' of the Pont du Gard had astonished and enchanted him.

Franklin was less interested in works of aesthetic genius than, usually, in human beings; and for the English – he had always been happy among them, however, much he detested the 'stupid brutal Opposition' the Colonists had met with from the obscurantist British government and their misguided sovereign – he had never ceased to feel a high regard:

'Of all the enviable things England has [he once told his London landlady] I envy it most its People. Why should a petty Island, which, compared to America, is but like a stepping Stone in a Brook, scarce enough of it above Water to keep one's Shoes dry; why, I say, should that little Island, enjoy in almost every Neighbourhood more sensible, virtuous and elegant Minds than we can collect in ranging 100 leagues of our vast Forests?'

Although Franklin and Jefferson did not originate the 'new idea' that Saint-Just acclaimed in 1794, they and the other authors of the Declaration gave it a fresh and stimulating turn. Since happiness was an 'inalienable right', those who pursued it were merely claiming a privilege that belonged to all mankind. Government, Jefferson believed, was 'a necessary evil* . . . a practical arrangement for securing at any time . . . the greatest happiness possible for the individual citizen.' With this view the cold-blooded visionary Saint-Just would have at least pretended to agree. While he did his ferocious work, he seems never to have lost hope that, by ridding the world of its 'tyrants', he laid the foundations of a modern terrestrial paradise, where the men and women he had released from servitude, and who could now be trusted to obey their own virtuous instincts, might live both happily and freely.

Having completed his mission, Franklin bade France a reluctant goodbye in the summer of 1785; and his departure was triumphal. As a parting gift, he was granted a mark of favour customarily reserved for ministers plenipotentiary if they had signed a treaty with the French government – a miniature of Louis XVI encircled by more than four hundred diamonds; and, on his way to Le Havre, he occupied one of Marie-Antoinette's luxurious curtained litters. Home at last in Philadelphia, he quietly settled down to a philosophic old age. The imminence of death seemed not to trouble him greatly:

'Being now in my 83rd year [he told Madame Brillon] I do not expect to continue much longer a Sojourner in this World, and begin to promise

* Karl Marx, of course, also looked forward to the supersession of the state which, although unavoidable in present conditions, would begin to wither away once class differences had been abolished by the proletarian revolution; until, during the 'final phase of communism', it had completely disappeared.

myself much Gratification of my Curiosity in soon visiting some other. Where-ever I may hereafter travel, be assured, my dear Friend, that . . . the Remembrance of your Friendship will be retained, as having made too deep an impression to be obliterated, and will ever, as it always has done, afford me infinite Pleasure. Adieu. Adieu.'

Although he believed in the immortality of the soul, Franklin's religious views were never wholly orthodox; and he admitted, not long before his death on August 13th, 1790, that he respected the moral teaching of Christianity, but was still inclined to question the divinity of Christ. During his last twelve months on earth, as he calmly awaited the end, he was only seriously disturbed by what he heard and read of 'the Misunderstandings and Troubles that have arisen in the Government of that dear Country, in which I pass'd nine of the happiest Years of my Life'; and he felt a deep sympathy for the beloved friends he had left behind there. The news that reached him from France had been 'very affecting'; but, luckily, he did not live to observe, even at a distance, the terrible progress of the Revolution and the advent of the Terror.

Jefferson, who died in 1826, and whose links with France had been far less personal, though he deplored the crimes committed in the Republic's name maintained that its cause was still the cause of freedom, and accepted Washington's view that, during the struggle between Great Britain and revolutionary France, the attitude of the United States must be strictly neutral. Then, early in 1794, he announced that he was resigning from public life and retired temporarily to the classic country house* that, after a careful study of Palladio, he had built on a Virginian hill-top. His decision was accompanied by a letter he addressed to James Madison, where he both explained his motives and gave a definition of the spiritual benefits he now expected to enjoy.

In the history of our subject his letter deserves to take its place beside the Declaration that he had helped to frame. 'Age, experience & reflection', he wrote, had induced him to set a higher value on tranquillity, now that 'the motion of my blood no longer keeps time with the tumult of the world', and had led him 'to seek for happiness in the lap and love of my family, in the society of my neighbours & my books, in the wholesome occupations

* 'Monticello' had been built in 1770.

[52]

of my farm and my affairs.' As a public personage, he added, he was obliged to give up everything he loved for everything that he detested; and he now felt confident – here, it seems, he was echoing Rousseau's *Promeneur Solitaire* – that he would find the tranquillity he sought in his garden and his fields, 'in an interest or affection in every bud that opens, in every breath that blows around me, in an entire freedom of rest or motion, of thought or incognitancy, owing account to myself alone of my hours and actions'. Jefferson, however, unlike Rousseau, could not finally resist his age; he preferred public usefulness to private happiness and, having re-entered politics, became the third President of the United States on March 4th, 1801.

4

'The Courage to be Happy'

URING the early nineteenth century, two distinguished French-men, having weathered the Revolutionary storm found the problem of human happiness particularly absorbing. Joseph Joubert had been born in 1754, his friend François René de Chateaubriand in 1768; and, although their lives were often closely linked, and each studied the other's character with appreciative attention, both of them very soon recognised how considerably they differed. Joubert, who lived until 1824, belonged to the eighteenth century and had inherited its respect for restraint and moderation, whereas Chateaubriand, who died nearly half-way through the nineteenth, witnessed first the rise and then the slow decline of the great Romantic Age that, in his heyday, he had once led. Joubert was an Epicurean philosopher, who set out to define and conquer happiness; Chateaubriand believed that Man's unhappiness was a proof of his spiritual distinction. 'Man,' he declared, 'you exist merely through suffering; you are nothing except for the sadness of your spirit and the eternal melancholy of your thought'.

Very different, too, were the attitudes they adopted towards the problem of the Self. Like Rousseau, Joubert was convinced that peace and self-regard – '*son repos et l'estime de soi-même*' – should be the individual's chief support, which one might achieve by 'living much with oneself, consulting oneself, listening to oneself'; while his friend, he wrote, soon after Chateaubriand published his immensely popular *Génie du Christianisme*, had, 'so to speak, all his faculties turned outwards . . . He

[54]

does not speak, with himself . . . never questions himself'; it was his readers' approval, rather than his own, he sought. 'Thus it follows that his talent will never make him happy . . .' As to his life, that was a different matter. There he remained the adventurous philanderer and Romantic egoist.* While he wrote for the benefit of others, and had his eye fixed upon his admiring literary audience, it was for himself alone he lived.

The contrast between the two writers became doubly apparent when they found they loved the same woman, and Chateaubriand's love was passionately returned, but Joubert had to be content with a tender *amitié amoureuse*, a gentle sisterly affection. Pauline de Beaumont belonged to an aristocratic family, the Montmorins, which the Revolution had cruelly broken up. Both her mother and her brother were guillotined; her father died during the hideous September Massacres. But the revolutionary commissioners, who threw Madame de Montmorin into the cart that carried her away towards her death, announced that Pauline was too weak to travel; and, although she tried in vain to run beside the wheels, she was eventually left behind. Her neighbour, Joubert, having heard her story, resolved that he would seek her out, and discovered her sitting before a cottage where she had taken refuge with a pair of kindly peasants.

Pauline was then twenty-six, Joubert already forty years old, a philosophic recluse, sensibly married to a modest, undemanding woman; and for Pauline he conceived a deep attachment that had some of the strength of a passion, but very little of a passion's turbulence and greed. His chief desire, since her worst sufferings had now passed, was to help restore her nearly broken spirit, and give her back the calm she needed. That, he suggested, was the only reward he sought. But, meanwhile, he must tell her, he wrote in 1795, he could not admire and respect her as much as he wished to do until she had shown the most beautiful form of courage, '*le plus beau de tous les courages*', the courage to be happy. She often despaired of life, and had told him that she would like to die quite alone at a village-inn on some casual expedition. A morbid fantasy, Joubert replied; to reach happiness,

---

* In his *Mémoires d'outre Tombe*, written many years after Joubert's death, Chateaubriand describes his old friend's preoccupation with himself, adding, however, that '*c'était un égoiste qui ne s'occupait que des autres*'.

she needed a determination to care for herself and a firm resolution that she would grow well. Pauline de Beaumont, however, whose health had always been frail, was at once a hypochondriac and a natural melancholic. Even before the Revolution destroyed her family, she had gone through an unhappy marriage. Now she proved a recalcitrant pupil; and, in the autumn of 1803, he was still affectionately scolding her.

Life, he asserted, was a duty of which we must do our best to make a pleasure, or, should it prove impossible, at least, '*un demi-plaisir*'. If that were the sole duty we had received from Heaven, we must discharge it calmly and gaily, and with as much grace as we could summon up, tending the sacred flame of existence and doing all we could to appreciate its warmth. When, at the start of the new century, Pauline fell wildly in love with the author of *Atala* – Chateaubriand's novel, she confessed, played on her nerves, like a hand playing on a clavecin – Joubert was alarmed and pained, yet sympathetic. The novelist, whom his circle nicknamed '*le Chat*', though already married, short, pock-marked and rather awkwardly built – '*un bossu sans bosse*', Madame de Lieven would presently observe – was known to exert a magnetic power over sensitive, impressionable women; and Joubert, being a perfectionist both in life and in literature, soon decided that sexual jealousy was the kind of vulgar emotion that a wise man carefully repressed. Once, invited with Madame Joubert to visit a house in the country that the lovers at the time were sharing, he took a volume of Kant, a philosopher he particularly disliked, to occupy his mind and strengthen his reserve, while he walked the garden paths beneath their windows.

Neither Joubert nor Chateaubriand could hope to save Pauline; but, during their efforts, each of them adopted a completely different method of approach. Joubert had demanded that she should strive against her unhappiness; Chateaubriand, who had ennobled the idea of suffering, tacitly accepted it. Pauline's spiritual woes reflected the human condition; and her physical fragility moved his heart. Her lack of any obvious appeal seems to have particularly attracted him; Madame de Beaumont, he wrote in his autobiography, was plain rather than beautiful – '*plutôt mal que bien de figure*'. Her face was thin and pale; and her almond-shaped eyes might perhaps have been too brilliant, had an air of extraordinary gentleness not

tempered the effect they made, just as a sunbeam is refracted and softened slanting through a glass of water.

During the early summer of 1803, Chateaubriand left for Rome, Napoleon, a great admirer of *Le Génie du Christianisme*, having, on Talleyrand's advice, appointed him First Secretary at the French Embassy; and Pauline, much to Chateaubriand's embarrassment and Joubert's dismay, insisted she would join him there. She arrived, totally exhausted after a long and difficult journey, and, on November 4th, died in her lover's arms. Chateaubriand's description of her last days, and particularly of her last attempt to enjoy the outer world, is one of his most moving literary flights. From the villa he had taken for her near the Spanish Steps, which she was rarely able to leave, they had visited the Colosseum. It had been a luminous autumn day; step by step, he tells us, she descended to the amphitheatre's lowest level, and there rested on a stone opposite a Christian altar. Naturally, the imaginative possibilities of the scene did not escape the great Romantic artist, as he watched her raise her eyes and let them stray round the gigantic cirque of ruins – stones that 'long had seen so much of death', now overgrown with brambles and saffron-yellow wild flowers – until they reached the altar and its marble cross, and she said, 'Let us go! I am feeling tired.'

Mourning became the author of *Atala*. 'Sorrow is my element', he had already informed Joubert. 'I only discover myself when I am unhappy'; and, although his friend's grief was equally poignant, it took a somewhat less dramatic shape. Soon after she had gained Rome, he wrote Pauline his last letter, dated October 12th, 1803:

'You bid me love you always [he reminded her]. Alas, can I do anything else, whatever you are, and whatever you may wish? Between us there was a sympathy, to which you have sometimes opposed many obstacles and contradictions . . . No one has ever inspired in me a more solid and faithful affection . . . Farewell, then, cause of such pain, who for me have been the source of so much good. Protect yourself; spare yourself; and come back into our midst one day, if only to give me, for a single moment, the indescribable pleasure of seeing you again'

Joubert shunned slavish displays of feeling; and, after Pauline's death, he assured the poet Chênedollé, a slightly more sympathetic figure than

Chateaubriand, that his sorrow was 'not extravagant', but, none the less, would be 'eternal'. Chateaubriand might 'regret her as keenly as I do', he said: 'but he will not miss her so long'. Then the passionate and the platonic lover each resumed his own career; Chateaubriand went on from triumph to triumph; Joubert continued to cultivate happiness, and presently built up another image that represented for him truth and beauty. Compared with his previous love, Louise de Vintmille was a bold, flamboyant personage – a thirty-nine-year-old *femme du monde*, partly Viennese by birth, who shone in fashionable Parisian society, was fond of fine clothes, silks and bright colours, and whose elderly husband wrote verses, which Joubert regularly took care to praise. She herself, though never a blue-stocking, had cultivated literary tastes. She was devoted to seventeenth-century literature, and claimed that she invariably went into mourning on the anniversary of Madame de Sévigné's death. Since she enjoyed excellent health, Madame de Vintmille, like her favourite authoress, could afford to temper wit with good nature. If a friend squinted, she once explained, she always looked at him or her in profile.

It was on July 22nd, 1802, that Joubert, who had originally met her among Pauline de Beaumont's friends, first began to feel her charm. He and Chateaubriand had walked at her side through the Gardens of the Tuileries; and he had halted to purchase her a huge bouquet of strongly-scented tuberoses – a flower that from that day would occupy as dominant a place in his sentimental recollections as cattleyas would long afterwards hold in the love-story of Odette and Swann. But the relationship that afterwards gradually developed, and was to last until his end, remained solely romantic and platonic, and derived its continued strength both from the delightful memories she evoked and that the fragrance of tuberoses unfailingly summoned up, and from the admiration he had always felt for her gay, untroubled spirit. His penultimate letter, written on the twentieth anniversary of their walk through the Gardens, when he knew that his end was drawing near and he could seldom venture out, refers to her equable nature, her perfectly sound judgement and, wherever she might be, the effect her 'laughing presence' made. She symbolised happiness, and the courage that happiness demands in a world of strife and discord.

During his lifetime, Joubert published nothing – he had luckily a small inherited fortune; and he wished, he wrote, to express no ideas 'unworthy of being inscribed either on silk or on bronze'. But his widow faithfully collected his manuscripts; and, fourteen years later, Chateaubriand edited and introduced them. It was a somewhat belated tribute, to which he added a characteristically melodious and lugubrious phrase; as he worked, he said, he had heard behind him the ebb and flow of memories that recalled the sound of a wave sweeping a faraway beach: '*J'écoute derrière moi les souvenirs, comme le bruissement de la vague sur une plage lointaine*' – an image probably inspired by the famous line of a Latin elegiac poet.* Chateaubriand had the misfortune to live too long, and thus witnessed the Revolution of 1848, which bewildered and appalled him. With the help of his servant, he still punctually climbed the stairs to the little salon kept by his last love, the septuagenarian beauty Madame Récamier, where he heard his memoirs read aloud. But he yearned, he said, to escape from a tormented world he could neither endure nor understand.

Chateaubriand's cult of sorrow was adopted by a succession of Romantic followers. Byron, oddly enough, mentions him only once – in a letter written soon after Waterloo, in which he refers to some anonymous verses on Napoleon's fall that he had sent to the editor of a London daily newspaper, and suggested they might perhaps appear '*as a translation* from some recent *French poetry* . . . It would not be bad fun to call it Chateaubriand's'; for 'the dog deserves no quarter . . .' Byron's animosity, of course, had a largely political origin; despite his much-advertised hatred of tyrants and tyranny, he continued to reverence the fallen Emperor; and the rival poet, having served under Napoleon, had issued, on the very day the victorious Allies entered Paris, a pamphlet welcoming home the Bourbons and defending the principles they represented. Yet the Englishman's literary self-esteem may also have played its part; Byron must surely have been well aware that between their two poetic heroes, Childe Harold and the Childe's predecessor René (who had fascinated Europe seven years earlier) there was an uncomfortably close relationship.

* Propertius: '*Litore sic tacito sonitus rarescit harenae*': 'So on the quiet shore does the sound of wave-swept sand grow fainter'.

Indeed, a shrewd biographer, Harold Nicolson, once told me that Byron, he believed, had never set foot in France because he was reluctant to enter his rival's territory, and preferred to dominate the literary stage alone.

Both Childe Harold and René are the enemies of happiness and have long abandoned its pursuit. Byron was the first Anglo-Saxon poet whose works had a strong, immediate, sometimes disruptive effect upon the existence of a whole generation, and not on critics and literati alone, but on an astonishing diversity of readers, who ranged from Madame de Lieven, the aristocratic Russian ambassadress, to a celebrated English courtesan, and, among the obscure, to 'a poor country girl' who begged for a lock of his hair, and a forlorn bankrupt, named Thomas Mulock, living in exile at Boulogne, who signed himself 'your Lordship's real Christian friend' and asserted that he was 'one of the few beings on earth who can understand the breadth and depth, and length and height, of your intellectual woes – one who has mourned and maddened where you now weep and writhe . . .'.*

The impression that *Childe Harold* made on Madame de Lieven, a woman much courted by George IV and a dazzling member of the clique that ruled Almack's Club, seems far stranger and more unexpected. In 1822, when, two years after the Regent's accession to the throne, she and husband were staying at the Brighton Pavilion – then a scene of profligate luxury, unparalleled, she thought, 'since the days of Heliogabalus' – she wrote to her faraway lover Prince Metternich, recalling a previous sojourn at the same resort. This had been in the summer of 1818; the third canto of *Childe Harold* had just appeared, and, as she was feeling dispirited and listless, she decided she would occupy her mind by attempting a translation:

'. . . I always took the poem with me when I went to sit on a certain rocky point, which is quite dry at low tide, but completely submerged at high. Lord Byron says terrible and sublime things about death by drowning, and I had always thought that passage particularly fine. I was reading it one day on the rocks; and I felt that nothing could be simpler than to stay on the point until the sea had covered it. I conceived the idea quite

* These, and many similar extracts from letters written by the poet's obscure admirers, are quoted in *To Lord Byron*, George Paston and Peter Quennell, 1939.

dispassionately. I cannot help believing . . . that we all have a certain tendency to madness . . . Evidently, my hour of madness had come. I experienced . . . nothing but a great unconcern in my heart and in my head. I waited on the rock a good half-hour . . . but the tide did not rise. When at last it did, my madness ebbed as the water advanced.'*

She had not even, she cheerfully assured Metternich, allowed the tide to wet her shoes; and she had burst out laughing on her way home; 'for, at that moment, nothing seemed so delightful as the small details of life, and nothing so stupid as the desire to die'. Madame de Lieven's suicidal impulse had lasted only half an hour; but there were other women – for instance, Caroline Lamb, Claire Clairmont and no doubt many less notorious votaries – who were made of feebler stuff, and whom their infatuation with Byron's 'demonic' genius would permanently bemuse and sometimes nearly destroy. To make his influence still more captivating, the sorrows of Childe Harold, and of Byron's other gloomy heroes, have almost always a mysterious origin. They arise from some unknown depth, and are part of a dark secret that the poet never quite divulges, and that his characters, he seems inclined to suggest, cannot completely understand themselves, though it visibly affects their conduct, and provokes the 'strange pangs' that, in the midst of his wildest dissipations, often 'flash along Childe Harold's brow'.

Not until Byron had reached Venice, and, free at last from the pall of gloom – 'the nightmare of my own delinquencies' – that had enveloped him since he left London, decided he would write a new poem, in which, he said, he meant 'to be a little quietly facetious upon everything', did his magnetic spell begin to wane. His closest friends, among them Hobhouse and Tom Moore, once they had seen the manuscript of *Don Juan*, were 'unanimous in advising its suppression'; they were shocked by his 'sarcasms upon his wife' (whom he caricatured as Juan's mother, Donna Inez), 'the indecency of parts . . . the attacks on religion . . . the abuse of other writers', and, above all perhaps, by the cheerful flippancy of the poet's tone, which replaced Childe Harold's brooding melancholy. After

---

* See *The Private Letters of Princess Lieven to Prince Metternich*, edited and translated by Quennell and Powell, 1937.

Don Juan's publication, many of his readers were astonished and disgusted; and his moral critics included the famous demi-mondaine Harriette Wilson. Since meeting him at a masked ball, she had long, she admitted, been 'sentimentally in love' with him, and had offered him her devoted friendship – which he had prudently declined, though, when she also begged his financial help, he had sent her fifty guineas. But now, having read *Don Juan*, she dashed off an indignant reprimand:

> 'Dear *Adorable* Lord Byron, *don't* make a mere *coarse* old libertine of yourself . . . I would not, even to *you* . . . lie under the imputation of such bad taste as to admire what in your cool moments, I am sure, you must feel to be *vulgar* at least . . .'

René's melancholy, like that of Childe Harold, was the attribute his admirers considered most attractive; and, again, its source remains mysterious, so long as the tragic secret that eventually drives him abroad, to live in the American forests amid the virtuous Indians, has not yet been laid bare. Until then, he suffers merely from an indefinable disquietude – a sense of loneliness, of ardent, unsatisfied yearnings, of the emptiness of mortal life, that has constantly pursued him. The only human being he truly loves is his sister Amélie; but she grows more and more evasive, and at last retires into a convent. There she sickens and dies, having, on her death-bed, uttered the few dreadful words that explain their joint tragedy – she has conceived a 'criminal passion' for the brother by whom she was innocently loved; and René then leaves Europe and takes refuge in the wilds of Louisiana, where, despite the comfort he has received from a venerable French priest and his good-hearted neighbours, he presently gives up the ghost.

René (which for Byron would one day have a special significance) appeared in 1805; the two opening cantos of *Childe Harold*, in 1812; and together they helped to launch the tide of melancholy feeling that rolls through nineteenth-century verse and prose. Romantic gloom was a very different emotion from many earlier forms of human sadness; it was more pervasive and had fewer obvious causes. In England during the sixteenth and seventeenth centuries, melancholy was often regarded either as spiritual sickness that might have a largely physical origin, or as a

deliberate manifestation of the sufferer's sense of wrong and of his private grievances against the world. Such social rebels, whom their happier contemporaries entitled 'malcontents', were easily recognisable when they stalked around the London streets, or skulked through the noisy crowd that filled St. Paul's, their arms folded, their hats pulled down towards their eyes, their hose, like Hamlet's, usually ungartered, wearing black cloaks, their rapiers reversed with the point thrust forward, and their right hands fingering their daggers.

Hamlet himself, superficially considered, is the type of malcontent; for the drama, as it now exists, is thought to have been based upon an old revenge-play popular about 1589, which Shakespeare adapted and, of course, wonderfully enlarged and subtilised. In the original play, the dispossessed Prince must also have adopted what Shakespeare's hero calls 'an antic disposition' and the gloomy trappings of a malcontent, mainly to disarm the suspicions of his wicked uncle's courtiers and guards; and John Marston's play *The Malcontent*, produced in 1604, shows the protagonist, Malevole, the ousted Duke of Genoa, who lives in disguise at the usurper's court, employing more or less the same stratagem. He performs his curious part well; he has become a surly exhibitionist. 'This Malevole', exclaims the reigning Duke, 'is one of the most prodigious affections that ever conversed with nature . . . his appetite is unsatiable as the grave; as far from any content as from heaven: his highest delight is to procure others vexation . . . the elements struggle within him; his own soul is at variance with itself . . .'

The Elizabethans and their immediate successors were fond of assuming a symbolic costume that revealed their inward feelings;* and although we know little else of the remarkable dramatist John Ford, whose master-piece, *'Tis Pity She's a Whore*, unfolds the tragic development of an incestuous passion, a single couplet dashed off by an unknown friend

* In *Twelfth Night*, Malvolio's yellow stockings indicate his passion for his mistress; while the Elizabethan diarist Thomas Wythorne, who also loved his employer, wore a russet suit, a colour that signified hope, and a garland of hops, which had the same significance, wreathed around his hat-brim.

> 'Deep in a dump John Forde was alone got
> With folded arms and melancholy hat'

— vividly suggests his character. An imaginary personage wearing the same kind of hat, his arms similarly folded, appears on the frontispiece of Richard Burton's *Anatomy of Melancholy*, the huge enyclopedic work that, after long research and some private experience of his subject, he published in 1621. Here he treats melancholy as a mental illness, of which love-melancholy is probably among the deadliest manifestations – even 'Fishes pine away for love' – and notes the various remedies that may perhaps effect a cure. They include the use of scents and regular scrubbings of the scalp. 'Odoraments to smell to, of rose water, violet flowers, bawme, rosecakes, vineger, &c. do much recreate the brains and spirits'; while irrigations of the shaven head, *'of the flowers of water lilies, lettuce, violets, camomile, wild mallows, wethers head, &c, must be used many mornings together'.*

Burton's learned advice shows that he thought of the dreaded disease as frequently remediable. Its name itself was derived from the Elizabethan theory that a man's character was determined not only by the mysterious influence of the stars, but by the results of the 'cardinal humour'* most effective in his constitution, melancholy's source being the 'Black Bile', which had subdued the livelier, more genial elements, but, given the right medicines, might presently be overcome. Melancholy, regarded as almost a virtue, as an interesting, even an appealing trait, was the conception of a later period. La Fontaine, during the second half of the seventeenth century, includes 'the sombre pleasure of a melancholy heart' among the assets of a civilised existence;† and, in English literature, Pope mentioned the 'not unpleasing melancholy' to which a sensitive poet now and then gave way. Once the first signs of the Romantic dawn had begun to appear on the horizon, it accompanied a passion for Gothic ruins and the more desolate aspects of Nature, and, entitled 'the Spleen', a variation of the

---

* The other humours, or 'chief fluids', were Blood, Phlegm and Choler. Black Bile was first thought to be the origin of 'sullenness and propensity to causeless and violent rages'; later, of 'mental gloom and sadness'.
† From La Fontaine's *Invocation* to the Spirit of Pleasure: *J'aime le jeu, l'amour, les livres, la musique, La ville et la campagne, enfin tout; il n'est rien Qui ne me soit souverain bien, Jusqu'au sombre plaisir d'un coeur mélancolique.*

disease that particularly attacked women, had a somewhat ludicrous and comic side.*

True, the Georgians, were also familiar with genuine melancholy at its ghastliest and darkest. Two distinguished poets William Cowper and William Collins were known to have gone melancholy mad; and, later, Collins' sighs and groans were daily heard resounding through the ancient cloisters of Chichester Cathedral; while Johnson and Boswell, we are often reminded, were racked by atrocious fits of gloom. But both the great man and his pupil deliberately sought for happiness – they were closer to Joubert than to Chateaubriand; and neither would have agreed that suffering was a badge of moral worth. They suffered despite themselves, and in their own lives accepted the human condition and its inescapable sorrows with all the fortitude that they could muster.

* See Pope's description in *The Rape of the Lock*, Canto IV, of Umbriel's descent into the Cave of Spleen, and of the Spirit who presides there:
> 'Hail wayward Queen!
> Who rule the Sex to Fifty from Fifteen,
> Parent of Vapors and of Female Wit,
> Who give th'*Hysteric* or *Poetic* Fit . . .'

5

```
'An Indissoluble Bond'
```

NEITHER happiness nor goodness is an attribute that novelists have found it easy to describe. Dickens' most praiseworthy characters are usually the least memorable; and the 'happy endings', with which he and his fellow Victorians frequently rounded off a story, when deserving personages are summoned back on to the stage, and each receives his or her appropriate reward, seldom satisfy a modern critic. One of the few convincing portraits of a really happy man has an unexpected origin; it comes from *Anna Karenina*, the book that Tolstoy, a far more determined moralist than Dickens – for whose genius, 'tinged with humour and melancholy', he had always felt a deep regard – wrote and published, first as an immensely popular serial, between 1873 and 1877. The heroine's brother, Stefan Arkadyevitch Oblonsky, has no obvious claim to approbation. He is happy because the happiness he enjoys, and very often spreads around him, is as much a part of his natural constitution as his height, the length of his arms, or the colour of his eyes. It is a quality that, despite occasional brief misgivings, he finds it almost impossible to overcome.

Yet *Anna Karenina*, in its dramatic entirety, has a strongly moral, indeed a profoundly pessimistic, theme. Under the grim epigraph, '*Vengeance is mine, and I will repay*', Tolstoy illustrates the disastrous effects of a consuming sexual passion. Desire gratified fails to bring happiness. When Vronsky first achieves his conquest of Anna, both are dreadfully transfigured. Tolstoy likens the lover to a frenzied assassin, who falls on

his victim's body, and 'drags it and hacks at it'. He covers her face and shoulders with kisses:

'All is over,' she said; 'I have nothing but you. Remember that.'
'I can never forget what is my whole life. For one instant of this happiness . . .'
'Happiness!' she said with horror and loathing, and her horror unconsciously infected him. 'For pity's sake, not a word, not a word more.'

Meanwhile Levin, the novelist's alter ego, takes a very different path. He loves a good, delightful girl, Kitty, Oblonsky's sister-in-law, whom, after a long and arduous courtship, he weds and carries off to his estate, where he hopes to reorganise his large neglected property and improve the condition of his backward peasant labourers. Levin is naturally serious and public-spirited. Yet the daily problems he encounters and, far worse, his spiritual anxieties and metaphysical doubts, soon undermine his peace of spirit; and, throughout his productive and apparently well-ordered marriage, there occur secret crises when, as Tolstoy had done, he feels so close to suicide that he hides the rope with which he might otherwise hang himself and, if he goes out into the fields and woods, prefers to leave his gun behind.

Against this turbulent background, Stefan Arkadyevitch goes his blithe, untroubled way. Critics have at times dismissed him as a mildly ridiculous *bon vivant*, who performs an amusing but unimportant rôle in this dark and complex story.* He is much more than that. Whenever he reappears, he changes the tempo of the narrative, for a while suspends its tragic course, and breathes an atmosphere of life and freedom. A trifler he may be, an Osric at the Russian Court. But he is not a fraud, still less a hypocrite – a fact that the novelist, though he detests every social standard his personage represents, sometimes readily acknowledges. 'Stefan

---

* A notable exception was Matthew Arnold, whose essay on Tolstoy, published in the second series of *Essays in Criticism*, 1888, contains a splendid tribute to Oblonsky. 'No, never, certainly,' writes Arnold, 'shall we come to forget Stiva'. Lionel Trilling, however, in *The Opposing Self*, 1955, mentions his name only once, and then does not discuss his personality.

Arkadyevitch', he admits, 'was a truthful man in his relations with himself', thus reminding us of the splendid advice that Polonius gives his son:

> 'This above all: to thine own self be true
> Thou canst not then be false to any man.'

Being true to himself, Stefan Arkadyevitch is false to no one, except, now and then, to his ageing wife Dolly; and, in that relationship, given their circumstances – his continued youth and Dolly's physical decline – the domestic fibs he is often obliged to tell her strike him as perhaps regrettable, yet also, he assumes, sadly unavoidable.

Anton Tchehov was a story-teller Tolstoy admired; and, in a criticism he published of *The Darling*, he suggested that its author, having first meant to 'knock down' his subject – a wonderfully affectionate but uncommonly stupid woman – at length had glorified and 'raised her up'. Tolstoy does not exalt Oblonsky – he cannot pretend that he approves of him; yet he credits the impenitent man of pleasure with a pervasive sheen or glow. Entering a fashionable restaurant beside this pleasant old friend, Levin notices 'a certain peculiarity of expression, as it were a restrained radiance, about the face and whole figure of Stefan Arkadyevitch. Oblonsky took off his greatcoat and, his hat over one ear, walked into the dining-room, giving directions to the Tatar waiters . . . Bowing to right and left . . . and here as everywhere joyously greeting acquaintances, he went up to the sideboard . . .'

Oblonsky's voice is one of his main assets; it is 'as soft and soothing as almond oil'; and his smile has a distinctive charm. When Levin begins gloomily discoursing on the imminence of death, Stefan Arkadyevitch gives a 'subtle and affectionate smile', which shows that, although he may not necessarily agree, he understands the other's feelings. An egoist by birth and education, he is neither insensitive nor hard-hearted. But deep misery and a sense of moral guilt, since he has never suffered from them himself, are quite beyond his comprehension; and, facing his wretched brother-in-law, Anna's cuckolded husband, he is utterly bewildered:

[68]

'"Alexey Alexandrovitch, believe me, she appreciates your generosity",
he said. "But it seems it was the will of God," he added, and as he said it
he felt how foolish a remark it was, and with difficulty repressed a smile
at his own foolishness.'

Anna he has already tried to cheer. She is ill and overwrought, he assures
her, and he hints, 'exaggerating dreadfully'. No one else in Stefan
Arkadyevitch's place, having to do with such despair, 'would have
ventured to smile . . . but in his smile there was so much of sweetness and
almost feminine tenderness that his smile did not wound'.

Among the dramatis personae of *Anna Karenina* Oblonsky occupies a
privileged position. His vices are implied; they need no underlining, and
are never harshly singled out as are the faults of other characters. Tolstoy
had an exceedingly close link with the men and women he created – with
Levin, especially, who embodied both his ideals and aspirations and many
of his own doubts and fears; with Vronsky, the military rake; and with
Anna herself, who, when he began work, was to have been an ugly but
attractive woman – she would have 'a narrow, low forehead' and 'a short,
turned-up nose', and only much later became a famous beauty – his
biographer tells us that he fell passionately in love. Stefan Arkadyevitch,
on the other hand, was his direct antithesis, a happy man, completely
unaware of the incessant spiritual problems that darkened his creator's
days.

While he wrote *Anna Karenina*, Tolstoy's own state of mind had been
particularly restless. There seemed, he announced during those years,
'nothing else to do in life but die . . . I am writing, I'm working very hard,
the children are healthy, but there is no happiness for me in any of it'. He
hated his chosen profession – 'writing corrupts the soul'; and he pretended
to condemn his book. 'What's so difficult', he enquired, 'about describing
how an officer gets entangled with a woman?' Such a description
demanded little skill, and served no kind of honest purpose. Yet Tolstoy's
portrait of Stefan Arkadyevitch is an imaginative masterpiece, where the
artist's gift of sympathising and understanding has surmounted every
obstacle that his moral prejudices raised. Although the novelist cannot

excuse his heroine, whose worst crime was that she had obeyed the dictates of a rebellious heart, but on whom the vengeance of Heaven must necessarily fall, her kinsman, an unfaithful husband and selfish spendthrift, never faces the divine tribunal; his hat over his ear, 'joyously greeting acquaintances' and giving directions to respectful waiters, he quietly circumvents his judges. Having lost one good official sinecure, he almost immediately finds a second; and we bid him a cheerful goodbye in the concluding chapter. 'There's my son-in-law,' remarks the old Prince, 'Stefan Arkadyevitch, you know him. He's got a place now on the committee of a commission and something or other . . . Only there's nothing to do in it . . . and a salary of eight thousand.'

Tolstoy's personage has clearly a comic side. In his portrait there is something of a patrician Micawber, another resolutely pleasure-seeking man, and, now and then, a touch of Falstaff. The moralist would later revile Shakespeare – Hamlet's 'affectations', for instance, repelled him; but Stefan Arkadyevitch has a true Shakespearian quality; and Hazlitt's eloquent description of Falstaff might almost equally well be a summing-up of Tolstoy's delightful anti-hero. 'His body', wrote the critic (an artist who hungered after happiness, but, alas, very seldom experienced it) 'is like a good estate to his mind, from which he receives rents and revenues of profit and pleasure'; and it is through the equable relationship he has established between mind and body that Falstaff derives 'an absolute self-possession, which nothing can disturb. His repartees are involuntary suggestions of his self-love; instinctive evasions of everything that threatens to interrupt the career of his triumphant jollity and self-complacency.'

Each character has taken his own measure. Surrounded by idealists, romantics, planners, political intriguers and militant 'iron men', he is perfectly content with the human happiness he finds in his day-to-day existence. Falstaff, however, has also a keen imagination and a retentive memory – 'We have heard the chimes at midnight, Master Shallow', he reminds his prosy old acquaintance – and, for all his rampant egotism, an unquestionably warm heart. He loves his callous young patron, as Shakespeare perhaps had loved his golden youth; and Falstaff's victorious career is only cut short when Henry, having just ascended the throne, cruelly compares him to an unclean figment of his own imagination:

'I know thee not, old man. Fall to thy prayers . . .
I have long dream'd of such a kind of man,
So surfeit-swelled, so old, and so profane;
But, being awak'd, I do despise my dream.'

Falstaff rallies, but soon dies. 'The King has killed his heart' laments the ever-loyal Mistress Quickly.

Euphoric characters like Falstaff and Stefan Arkadyevitch are not prone to self-analysis – their greatest strength is that they take happiness as it comes, and accept it almost as a birthright. Thus they have rarely attempted to portray themselves. But there is one magnificent exception. The diary of Samuel Pepys contains the self-portrait of a man who shared some of their tastes and many of their psychological advantages, and avoided most of the lasting conflicts by which other personalities have been undermined. Not that he escaped anxieties and afflictions, or lacked at times a sense of sin; but, throughout the whole *Diary*, although he remained persistently introspective, and never minimised his faults and failures, records of happiness predominate. Here the knowledge that he had succeeded in life evidently assisted him. The son of a London tailor, but luckily a cousin of Lord Sandwich, he had soon developed into an ambitious and efficient civil servant, determined, while he did his duty, to get on in the world and improve his social and financial status, until, at last, he found himself walking and talking familiarly with the rulers of the kingdom.

We still admire the splendid variety of Pepys' lifelong tastes and interests; and, when he left the world in 1703, his old friend and fellow diarist John Evelyn paid him the tribute he deserved: 'This day dyed Mr. Sam: Pepys, a very worthy, Industrious and curious person, none in England exceeding him in the Knowledge of the Navy . . . universaly beloved, Hospitable, Generous, Learned on many things, skill'd in Musick, a very great cherisher of Learned man . . .'. By 'curious', of course, Evelyn meant that Pepys' desire for knowledge about any subject that he undertook, from ship-building to the arts and sciences – he would one day be elected President of the newly-founded Royal Society – was extraordinarily wide-

ranging. But, at the same time, unlike many scientifically-minded men, he was devoted to the spectacle of life as it passed beneath his eyes. Every observation he could make, whether it was of his own frequently ill-advised and, now and then, discreditable behaviour, or of the traits of famous public personages, invariably delighted him. During the early summer of 1660, for example, when he accompanied Charles II back to England, he had watched the King on deck:

'. . . We weighed Ancre, and with a fresh gale . . . we set sail . . . all the afternoon the King walking here and there, up and down (quite contrary to what I thought he had been) very active and stirring'.

Later, as the royal procession landed:

'I went, and Mr Mansell and one of the King's footmen, with a dog that the King loved (and which shit in the boat, which made us laugh and me think that a King and all that belong to him are but just as others are) . . .'

Although Pepys is usually most likeable if he conveys the satisfaction he derived from living, even in his darkest private crises, a reader may sometimes assume, he half enjoyed the drama of the scene, as when his wife, distracted by jealousy because she had caught him fondling her maid, threatened him in bed with a pair of red-hot tongs; 'at which I rose up, and with a few words she laid them down and little by little, very sillily, let all the discourse fall; and about 2 . . . came to bed and there [we] lay well all night . . . talking together with much pleasure . . .' Pepys was a deeply attached, but regularly unfaithful, husband; and he, too, having conceived a wild suspicion that Mrs Pepys had become enamoured of her new dancing-master, Mr Pembleton, 'a pretty neat black man', grew 'so deeply full of jealousy . . . that I could not do any business; for which', he wrote a day later, 'I deserve to be beaten, if not really served as I am fearful of being; especially since, God knows, that I do not find enough honesty in my own mind but that upon a small temptation I could be false to her, and therefore ought not to expect more from her – but God pardon both my sin and my folly therein.'

Women and music, he had discovered at an early stage of his life, were his most deeply rooted passions. The first he did not hesitate to satisfy, though often in circumstances that did him little credit; and if he could combine the two, and enjoy the proximity of women while he listened to good music, or sang and played it himself, his satisfaction was unlimited. 'Pleasure' is a word that occurs repeatedly in his account of how he had passed the previous day. Thus, on April 8th, 1667, he and his wife, having begun the evening with a dinner party of twelve and a visit to the King's playhouse, and thence to see the Italian puppets, where they had 'three times more sport than at the play', they returned to their own garden, 'the first night we have been this year'; and the four of them – besides the Pepyses, Mercer, Elizabeth Pepys' companion, in whom her employer took an amorous interest, and her successor, 'our Barker' – all sat up late 'singing very well', and then supper and so to bed. He was 'mightily pleased with this day's pleasure', the happy diarist concludes.

We read of many such earlier and later feasts. In March 1669, to take a single occasion, once 'our music came' and candles had been lit, Pepys, his wife, a group of friends and two strange gentlemen he had casually invited, 'fell to dancing and continued only with intermission for a good supper, till two in the morning', accompanied by a 'most excellent violin and theorbo, the best in town; and so, with mighty mirth and pleased with their dancing of Jiggs', of which the last performers were 'W. Batelier's* blackmore and blackmore maid; and then to a country-dance again; and so broke up with extraordinary pleasure, as being one of the days and nights of my life spent with the greatest content, and that which I can but hope to repeat . . . a few times in my whole life.'

Pepys' most memorable account of a happy day, however, is surely his description of a jaunt to Epsom in July, 1667. Not only is it a vivid piece of simple descriptive writing; but it illustrates some of the characteristics on which his happiness was based – his affection for, and sympathy with, his fellow men, his gift of observation, his love of beautiful things and his imaginative interest in the past. Although earlier that day he had sprained his right foot by leaping a little bank, it had very soon recovered; and he led

* William Batelier was a prosperous London wine-merchant.

his companions, Elizabeth Pepys, a Mr and Mrs Turner and Will Hewer, his devoted clerk, on a walk across the downs:

'... where a flock of sheep was, and the most pleasant and innocent sight that ever I saw in my life; we find a shepheard and his little boy reading ... the Bible to him. So I made the boy read to me, which he did with the forced tone that children do usually read, that was mighty pretty; and then I did give him something and went to the father and talked with him ... He did content himself mightily in my liking the boy's reading and did bless God for him, the most like one of the old Patriarchs that ever I saw in my life, and it brought those thoughts of the old age of the world in my mind for two or three days after. We took notice of his woolen knit stockings of two colours mixed, and of his shoes shod with Iron ... with great nails in the soles ... "Why", says the poor man, "the Downes you see, are full of stones ... and these ... will make the stones fly till they sing before me" ... He values his dog mightily, that would turn a sheep any way ... [He] told me there was about 18 score sheep in his flock, and that he hath 4s a week the year round for keeping of them.'

It is typical of Pepys that the happiness this episode gave him should have been derived from a host of different details – not only from the 'forced tone' in which the shepherd-boy read aloud and the vision of the shepherd as a relic of the ancient world that haunted him, he tells us, for several days, but from the structure of the old man's shoes and the exact amount of a trusted servant's wages, the latter being the kind of solid information he always carefully recorded. Here he much resembled Samuel Johnson, to whom no scrap of knowledge came amiss if it increased his understanding of the world. Like Johnson, too, he needed company, and was usually happiest among his friends. Both men loved the stimulus of social life and had little taste for solitude, a condition the Romantics would deliberately seek. Even a cat, Johnson pointed out to Hester Thrale, never purrs when it is quite alone; and, during the seventeenth and eighteenth centuries, civilised men and women were evidently a great deal more gregarious, more addicted to amusements they could share, than they have become today.

Hence their love of parties. The entertainments they arranged and attended took extremely various forms. Now they might join a simple domestic gathering such as the Vicar of Wakefield and his family enjoyed in a newly-reaped meadow: 'we sat, or rather reclined, round a temperate repast, our cloth spread upon the hay ... To heighten our satisfaction, two blackbirds answered each other from opposite hedges ...' Now, if they belonged to the 'polite world', they would appear at one of the fashionable routs, blue-stocking assemblies, balls, concerts and bohemian masquerades that diversified the London season. Here another self-portraitist throws a brilliant light upon the social habits of his age; William Hickey's *Memoirs*, which he began to write about 1808 or 1809, depict the progress of a particularly gregarious man, who, although beside Pepys he may seem a somewhat undistinguished character, was equally energetic, no less fond of life and just as determined to squeeze out of existence every drop of interest and enjoyment that it could be made to yield.

Not until he had abandoned an active career did he finally turn to remembering and writing; and then it was forced upon him by lack of suitable companionship. Once he left India, where he had long practised the law and had earned a fortune that, if not very large by Anglo-Indian standards, was quite sufficient for his purpose, he had settled in a small but comfortable house in the little Buckinghamshire town of Beaconsfield, whence he visited nearby friends and, every six weeks or so, 'ran up to London', the scene of his adventurous childhood and boisterous, undisciplined youth. After a time, however, this prosaic routine lost its charm. Beaconsfield, he decided, was a sadly 'trifling place' and, worse still, had a 'very limited society'. He suffered from dreadful headaches, and presently, from 'my old disagreeable nervous sensations' that even an 'affectionate' and attentive doctor could not wholly cure.

Meanwhile, reliving the past helped him 'fill a painful vacuum' on days when the English climate or some minor malady made it impossible for him to leave the house; and the huge self-portrait he drew – the original manuscript of his memoirs runs to seven hundred and forty-four pages* – enlarged its scope year after year. Son of a prosperous Irish lawyer, who

* It has never been published in full; but between 1913 and 1925 the late Alfred Spencer edited a four-volume selection of the text, while I was responsible for the single-volume edition that came out, with less material but fewer expurgations, in 1950.

had belonged to Samuel Johnson's circle, Hickey was very much a man of his age, and, in his opinion at least, essentially an *homme du monde*. He had also been, even during his boyhood, a keen frequenter of the *demi-monde*; for his raffish elder brother Henry had introduced him to 'many of the gay adventurers of London, men who lived by their wits; that is nobody knew how . . . with all of whom I . . . was in high favour, and many a bumper of champagne and claret have I drank in the society of this set, at taverns and brothels, accompanied by the most lovely women of the metropolis, and this before I had completed my fourteenth year'.

Hickey's outlook, it soon becomes apparent, was far narrower and more philistine than that of Pepys; he had little of Pepys' learning and good taste, never mentions a book he has read or a work of art that he has seen. What he admired, and sought to achieve in his surroundings, was an air of smartness, neatness, ship-shapeness and general luxury and elegance. His favourite laudatory adjectives were 'rich', 'capital', 'magnificent', 'choice' and 'fine'. He purchased gaudy clothes – so gaudy that they were sometimes laughed at when he exhibited them in public – and was always fond of bright colours. When he and seven like-minded friends bought and fitted out a cutter for expeditions on the Thames, 'she was painted', we learn, 'a bright azure blue, with gold mouldings and ornaments . . . richly embellished with aquatic devices. The awning was of the same colour, in silk, as were the dresses of the eight rowers, their jackets and trousers being trimmed with an uncommonly neat spangle and foil lace . . . We wore black round hats with very broad gold bands and small bright blue cockades . . . Under the awning we had capital French horns and clarinets . . .'

To a robust appetite for the transitory pleasures of life Hickey added strong nerves and an extremely vigorous constitution – so many children then died in infancy that the survivors were usually made of very solid stuff, or possessed a mysterious inward strength that enabled them to develop, like Horace Walpole, into Herculean invalids. Tolstoy's admirable portrait of Stefan Arkadyevitch Oblonsky and Pepys' and Hickey's vivid self-portraits lead us gradually towards the same conclusion: a gift for happiness may often be an attribute, closely bound up, no doubt, with certain physical traits, that Nature bestows on some human beings, and unaccountably denies to others; and, when George Washington,

delivering his Inaugural Address in 1789, announced that there was 'an indissoluble bond between virtue and happiness', and Aristotle, during the fourth century before Christ, proclaimed that happiness resulted from 'the active exercise' of virtue, they seem both of them, although with the noblest intentions, to have grievously misled their hearers.

6

Seeing and Recording

I N 1845, at the age of twenty-six, John Ruskin was allowed for the first
time to visit Switzerland, the country where he had always felt
happiest, as an independent traveller. Yet, although on this occasion
neither his mother nor his father accompanied him, he was still attended by
a Swiss courier named Couttet and George, his faithful English valet; and
one day, while he climbed a mountain-slope, he heard his guardians, who
had fallen a little behind, talking of their young employer. '*Le pauvre enfant,
il ne sait pas vivre!*' remarked the courier to the valet – a not unjust criticism,
with which Ruskin would probably have agreed. He was then suffering
from the after-effects of an unhappy love affair; and in all the relationships
that followed he was to show the same distressful lack of worldly
knowledge. His emotions persistently overcame his reason; the ability to
live happily as a man among men was an art he never wholly mastered.

Yet he survived until the opening of the next century; and before he
reached middle age, despite the frustrations and miseries he endured, he
had already realised his genius and fulfilled his early promise. This he
accomplished through the use that he made of his eyes. Seeing, he often
assured his readers, was the 'greatest thing' a human soul could do.* We
must be constantly *looking* – at alder-stems, 'covered with the white
branchy moss' that so much resembled twigs of coral; the 'intense scarletty

---

* This belief is echoed by Thomas Carlyle, who is seldom regarded as an aesthete: 'No
most gifted eye can exhaust the significance of any object'.

[78]

purple' of shattered larch-boughs; the polished boulders in an Alpine torrent; or, above our heads, the 'long, continuous and delicate formation' of a swelling cloud. Only Chateaubriand has so brilliantly described clouds; and *Modern Painters*, the book of which Volume I had appeared in 1843, contains a memorable paragraph where he distinguishes between the varying shapes that they assume, from the 'colossal mountain of grey cumulus', and the 'quiet multitudes of the white, soft, silent cirrus', to the rain-cloud with its 'veily transparency' and its 'ragged and spray-like edge'.

As an art-critic, Ruskin frequently became a moralist, who asserted that part of a picture's value might depend on the moving story the painter illustrates or the salutary message he expounds. None the less, particularly during his middle years, the critic was simultaneously an imaginative hedonist; and the observation of beauty, pursued for its own sake, provided nearly all the satisfactions that life had otherwise refused him. The chief purpose of any true work of art, he perceived, was primarily to cause pleasure by conveying the creative delight that the artist had himself enjoyed; and, with the passage of time, Ruskin grew more and more reluctant to reject a work simply because he disapproved of its social or its moral background. Thus, he detested the age to which Paolo Veronese had belonged, and the 'corrupt' and 'decadent' architecture of sixteenth-century Venice, yet loved Veronese's sensuous warmth and ebullient humanity – 'Paolo', he said, 'is as full of mischief as an egg is full of meat'; and he believed, he assured a friend, that 'after all, you'll find the subtlest and grandest *expression* . . . hidden under the gold and purple of those vagabonds of Venetians'.

Unselfishness was a virtue that had constituted the basis of his education. But he now discovered that it did not always make for happiness or, indeed, for health and calm. If he worked selfishly, observed and drew and bought the pictures he admired, he was 'happy and well; but when I deny myself . . . and work at what seems useful, I get miserable and unwell . . . Everything that has turned out well I've done merely to please myself, and it upsets all one's moral principles. Mine are going I don't know where.' In fact, the hedonist would never vanquish the moralist; as Ruskin grew older, he became increasingly concerned with the betterment of mankind.

But, meanwhile, his health deteriorated and his grasp on sanity weakened, until, at the end of his life, even Turner's luminous sketches that covered his walls and the landscape that lay beyond his windows had lost their power to raise his spirits. Both had faded; for, he admitted, quoting sadly from *The Tempest*, 'all the best of this sort are but shadows'.

Although Ruskin cannot himself be regarded as an example of the happy man – at some moments, no doubt, he was unusually wretched – he acquired and practised one of the noblest gifts that have ever contributed to happiness, the gift of seeing, and sometimes recording, the beauty and wonderful variety of the universe into which we have been born. A modern writer, the late Norman Douglas, announced that he would rather have been blind than deaf; but, if we except musicians and musicologists – and some of the latter I have heard admit that they derived just as much enjoyment from *reading* a score as from listening to a piece of music played – surely no intelligent man today could hold the same eccentric view. For every good painter and almost every imaginative writer, close and accurate observation has been throughout their lives a ruling passion, which, unlike so many passions, has had the happiest results.

Diaries left by famous artists are full of the verbal sketches they have jotted down. Both Eugène Delacroix and John Constable – a fellow-artist Delacroix greatly admired – enliven their pages with such detailed notes. The French painter, though naturally drawn towards huge and grandiose subjects, studied a garden slug with as keen and appreciative an eye as elsewhere he turned on an imprisoned lion. Of the lions, watched during a heat-wave at the Jardin des Plantes, 'I managed to observe [he records] that . . . the light tone visible beneath the stomach, under the paws, etc., is merged more softly into the rest than I usually make it . . . the colour of the ears is brown, but only on the outside.' Of the slug's colouration, he was equally observant; it was 'spotted like a jaguar, with broad rings upon its back and sides, turning into single spots on the head and near the stomach, where it was lighter in tone, as in quadrupeds'.

Constable, too, made an intense preliminary study of every landscape or object that he painted; and, before he began work, 'the first thing I try to do', he said, 'is *to forget that I have ever seen a picture*'. Having thus cleared his mind of preconceptions, he became completely self-absorbed; and his

[80]

biographer Charles Leslie reports, as 'a curious proof of the stillness with which he sat', that, one day while he was working in the open air, a field mouse was found to have crept into his coat-pocket. But, besides observations, Memory played a part. Sights and sounds that had once fascinated his boyhood – 'the sound of water escaping from mill-dams . . . willows, old rotten planks, slimy posts and brickwork' – still excited his imagination. The technical expert who, when he was about to hang a picture, might be seen at the last moment, with the help of a palette-knife and a mysterious liquid he had himself compounded, putting on what he called its 'dewy freshness', was above all else a visionary artist.

'Painting is with me,' he announced to a friendly correspondent, 'but another word for feeling'; and that feeling, from what we know of his work and table-talk, must have brought him, so long as his beloved wife still lived and he preserved his aesthetic self-confidence, deep and well-deserved joy. He shunned melancholy, detested Byron's verse, and seems to have enjoyed romantic exaltation, yet escaped the influence of Romantic gloom. His earlier pictures reflect his own contemplative serenity. But then, after all, there is no major work of art, however grim or tragic its theme,* that does not transmit something of the artist's pleasure in his work to even the least curious and most casual observer.

Many years ago, at a Japanese university,† I caused a good deal of consternation among my students and colleagues by suggesting that the enjoyment we derived from a book or a picture was the true basis of critical appreciation, and that, having first enjoyed, we should next, like Baudelaire discussing Wagner's music, 'investigate the *why*', and seek 'to turn our pleasure into knowledge'. Most Western critics today would admit the importance of the pleasure principle, and have discarded the early-twentieth-century belief that 'significant form', 'rhythmic unity', 'plastic sensibility', and sometimes 'inner tension', are necessarily the hallmarks of a painting's value. In his admirable book *Looking at Pictures*, Kenneth Clark, a pupil of Roger Fry, who, he declared, had originally taught him 'how to look', dwells both on the merits of a picture's

* For example, Géricault's *Raft of the Medusa* or Goya's *The Third of May.*
† *The Marble Foot,* 1976.

composition and on the subject the artist has chosen and the experience of human life it unmistakably reveals.

Our ability to share and re-live that experience is one of the delights of seeing – for example, when, at London's Kenwood House, we confront Rembrandt's splendid self-portrait. Our first thought, Kenneth Clark writes, 'is of the soul imprisoned in that life-battered face . . . it is primarily the record of an individual soul', and, we immediately note, a tragic record. Rembrandt's head is very far from handsome; the nose is bulbous and red-blotched; the cheeks are rugged and sagging; heavy wrinkles score the forehead. Nor is the expression calm; it betokens determination and immense creative strength, a kind of fierce pride, but not the smallest hint either of personal equanimity or of professional self-satisfaction.

It is by no means a 'pretty picture'; and in its neighbourhood hangs one of the prettiest and most vivacious portraits that Thomas Gainsborough ever painted – the likeness of a dashing, elegantly dressed young woman who trips across a pastoral landscape. The hurried visitor immediately succumbs to her charm. Rembrandt attracts a less enthusiastic crowd. Yet it is the self-portrait – the ugly scarred face with its severe background, which consists of two half-circles apparently traced on the wall – that always draws us back again. Rembrandt's record of his vexed, tormented soul is far more deeply and enjoyably moving than Gainsborough's vision of carefree youth and fashionable grace.

The state of mind that a masterpiece helps us enjoy no doubt has many different causes. Among them is the pleasure of recognition; the work that confronts us somehow satisfies our sense of *rightness*; we find there the strange quality, indefinable yet inescapable, that distinguishes a work of art from a mere commercial counterfeit. It is an exposition of truth as an artist himself sees it; and in his self-portrait Rembrandt tells us the whole truth about his individual knowledge of the world, about the sorrows of age, the woes of poverty and failure. The marvellous frankness with which he lays his soul bare simultaneously warms the beholder's heart and quickens his intelligence. '*Il y a de l'oraison en toute grande oeuvre*' – there is a hymn of praise in every great work – believed the French religious thinker Alain; and, though Rembrandt's picture has no devotional message, it seems to voice an artist's gratitude for life, for the gifts that, despite the

[82]

Rembrandt's self-portrait 'tells us the whole truth about his individual knowledge of the world'.

hardships he has undergone, have enabled him to remain so very much himself. When he painted it, during the early 1660s, he was near the conclusion of his fifth decade – he would die in five or six years' time – a lonely figure, who had long outgrown his earlier wealth and popularity, but never lost touch with the satisfaction of working or a spontaneous zest for living.

Although Rembrandt was an extraordinarily individual artist, he paid close attention to the works of other men, studied the techniques employed by previous painters, sketched Roman busts and collected and copied Indian miniatures. Any discovery we make, if it provides some new insight into art or life, is usually stirring and refreshing; and to discover the connection between different artists, which emphasises the recurrent patterns of life and the continuous growth of art itself, as it has developed since the Neolithic Age, almost invariably gives us pleasure. Not long ago, for example, by a 'happy chance' – to use the adjective's original meaning – I opened a fine new picture book* – where I found a photograph of Mantegna's *Presentation of Christ* that reminded me of a 'Florentine painted terracotta relief, attributed to Donatello', then being exhibited at a London saleroom.

Mantegna, I next learned, had met Donatello during a visit to Padua, and later, in 1485, 'was to paint a *Virgin and Child* (Brera, Milan) surely dependent' on one of Donatello's works. Between Mantegna's *Presentation* and Donatello's terracotta relief there is a curious resemblance. Mantegna's handling of his subject is peculiarly his own. Each of the six personages represented has a separate attitude towards this memorable occasion. The Child has begun to cry; the High Priest appears to feel its sacredness; but two minor characters, on the left and the right, have a cool, uninterested look;† while the Virgin holds out her swaddled child with an air of suppliant reverence. She has a beautiful face, which, it soon occurred to me, was somehow pleasantly familiar. Had she not a fascinating likeness

* *The Bible and its Painters*, by Bruce Bernard, with an introduction by Laurence Gowing, 1983. Mantegna's picture is now in the Staatliche Museum, West Berlin.
† The figure on the right is a self-portrait; that on the left, gazing into vacancy, his wife, the sister of Giovanni and Gentile Bellini.

to Donatello's pensive Virgin? They have the same narrow downcast eyes, the same poetic line of mouth and chin, even the same slightly tip-tilted nose.* Since the artists, when they met at Padua, no doubt exchanged ideas, may they not have used as their model the same Italian peasant-girl? The knowledge that they had a close and productive relationship certainly adds to our enjoyment of their work.

Meanwhile, I have sometimes wondered if the pleasure of looking at pictures, and studying the relationship of artists, is today really much more general than it was a hundred years ago. The human race might still be roughly divided into two opposing groups – those for whom seeing is a workaday function that helps them guide their steps from hour to hour, and those for whom the visual images they receive are a major source of happiness. '. . . Man has closed himself up', wrote Blake in *The Marriage of Heaven and Hell*, 'till he sees all things thro' the narrow chinks of his cavern'; and one need not be a Blakeian mystic, or believe that, were 'the doors of perception' cleansed, 'every thing would appear . . . as it is, infinite', to agree that, whether we are considering art or nature, or any single object we can examine through a fresh, unclouded eye, the precious gift of seeing, used with imagination, will effectively enlarge the cavern's chinks. A picture we call 'great' is the lasting record of such a visionary enlargement. An artist recreates the world; each painter has his own world; and to enter it, and admire its landscape, is always a memorable experience; so that looking at new pictures, in a gallery or on other people's walls, may from a pastime eventually become a passion. When I open the door of an unfamiliar room, my first impulse is to approach the pictures it encloses. Not only do they arouse my curiosity – in portraits, how extraordinarily compulsive an unknown face may be! – they raise my hopes of stepping across the margin of the frame into a country I have never visited before.

Some pictures seem especially designed to satisfy that aspiration. By popular German critics they are sometimes called 'walk-about-pictures'; and if there is a masterpiece that thoroughly deserves the title, it is Nicolas Poussin's glorious work, *The Body of Phocion carried from Athens*, painted

---

* In Donatello's bas-relief, I learn, the Virgin's robe has a rich pomegranate pattern that also appears on some of Mantegna's works.

Nicolas Poussin's glorious Athenian landscape is entirely the product of his own creative genius.

half-way through the seventeenth century. A companion-picture, *The Gathering of the Ashes of Phocion*, illustrates the same subject – the undeserved end of a valiant Athenian soldier, who, wrongly suspected of having betrayed his countrymen, was condemned, like Socrates, to drink the hemlock.

Each portrays a wide and airy landscape, supposed to be the neighbourhood of Athens. Poussin himself, born at Andelys on the banks of the Seine, could never have visited what was then the Turkish Empire; and, although he knew Italy well, the marvellous prospects he unfolds are neither Grecian nor Italian, but entirely the products of his own creative genius. Except for the frontage of a temple that overlooks the scene, most

[86]

details of the two landscapes, despite the fact that we observe them from an identical standpoint, are perplexingly dissimilar. In *Gathering the Ashes* behind the temple's façade rises a fantastic rocky peak, which in its companion has been replaced by an impressive circular tower. Even the tall trees on the left and right of the sinuous path that winds away towards Athens are of different forms and species. But, whichever picture we are examining at the time, that sinuous path tempts us to follow it until we have entered the Ideal City.

Should we yield to the temptation, we must expect a long walk; we shall pass more inhabitants of the place, out in the fields for the day, than we can reasonably attempt to count; and those who populate the landscape from which Phocion's corpse is being carried are particularly numerous. A peasant is shepherding his flock; two strange white-shrouded figures occupy a bullock-cart. Across the middle distance gallops a solitary red-cloaked horseman, and far off a long religious procession moves to the sound of music beneath the temple's walls. Though the trees are still in full leaf, the season is late summer or early autumn. The sun has begun to sink; an immense cumulus cloud drifts high overhead; and the city that climbs the hill beyond the temple, where its buff-coloured masonry catches the evening light, has an air of antique peace and splendour.

Many such imaginary cities emerge in the backgrounds of Renaissance pictures; and they, too, persuade us, once we have absorbed the main subject – a Virgin and Child, or Mantegna's vision of *The Agony in the Garden* – to move around and beyond it into a completely separate realm of feeling. A work of art, however, is not an escape-route from life, but provides a purification and vivid intensification of our everyday experience; and 'walk-about-pictures' are merely a single aspect of the search for happiness – if by 'happiness' we mean a sense of celestial harmony that inspires a painter's or a writer's efforts.

Some artists, of course, have been more alive to the search than others and pursued it more deliberately. Renoir, for example, having filled so many canvases with the scenes he liked best – plump, sleek girls sunning their naked bodies, or dancing and drinking with their lovers at a riverside restaurant – once protested that pictures of people whole-heartedly enjoying themselves were not always inferior as works of art to pictures of a more dramatic and heroic kind. Two other great eighteenth-century French artists, Fragonard and Chardin, in their very different ways were

almost equally concerned with a certain kind of sensuous bliss. Fragonard, a native of Provence, having won the Prix de Rome, which earned him a visit to Italy, had soon turned against the Old Masters. Michelangelo's energy 'terrified' him. Raphael moved him to tears; but 'the pencil fell from my hands' he wrote; and 'I remained for some months in a state of indolence that I lacked the strength to overcome'. Tiepolo was one of the few Italian artists whom he admired and understood.

It was the air of feminine elegance and underlying gaiety, with which the great Venetian managed to enliven his most ceremonious allegorical frescoes, that, no doubt, attracted Fragonard. Gaiety became the keynote of his genius; few eighteenth-century artists have had so light and elusive a touch, and, simultaneously, so affectionate an attitude towards every subject that they handled. Beside Fragonard, Watteau was a visionary melancholic; about his exquisite pastorals there is always a shade of sorrow; he is haunted by Beauty's evanescence and the fragility of human pleasures –

> '. . . Beauty that must die;
> And Joy, whose hand is ever at his lips
> Bidding adieu . . .'

as a carefree group prepares to embark for Cythera, or a single dancer moves across the lawn.

Fragonard's lyrical series, entitled *Le progrès de l'amour dans les coeurs des jeunes filles,** which Madame du Barry commissioned for her country house, but, after some disagreement, the artist took away with him to Provence to decorate his own walls, is by comparison a high-spirited tribute to Youth and Love at their most radiantly hopeful. Love, traversing the hearts of young girls, throws them into a dazzling confusion. One is apparently running for her life; yet, as she flees, both virginal arms extended, she glances back over her shoulder at the young man who stretches out his hand, not to grasp her skirts and violate her innocence, but simply to offer her a rose. It is a prearranged flight rather

* Now in the Frick Museum, New York.

[88]

than a genuine surprise; and two succeeding pictures, entitled 'The Declaration of Love' and 'The Lover Crowned', show that passion soon reaches its 'right true end' amid the classic urns, venerable garden-statues and huge umbrageous avenues of this long-lost Earthly Paradise.

Chardin, on the other hand, was perfectly content with his everyday domestic surroundings and the splendid discoveries he made there. Born in 1699, son of a successful carpenter who manufactured billiard-tables for the King, Jean-Baptiste-Siméon Chardin had begun his professional career as an assistant to other artists; but when his employer at the time, Noël-Nicolas Coypel, brother of the famous 'history-painter' Antoine Coypel, ordered him to paint a huntsman's gun, this commission, his first chance of painting directly from a homely natural object, had a liberating effect upon his genius. Then, in 1728, his still-life of a fishmonger's skate, *La Raie*, gained him admission to the Academy, where Largillière, after considering his works, assumed that they were excellent products of 'the Flemish School', and was astounded to learn that they were the achievements of a French artist. Chardin had quickly recognised his true vocation; and, ever since he exhibited *La Raie*, his vision of the world has been described and applauded by critics, among the earliest being Denis Diderot, one of the more recent Marcel Proust, who made him the subject of a long and moving early essay.*

The critic, Diderot wrote to Grimm in 1762, needed 'taste of many different kinds, a heart responsive to all delights and a soul capable of an infinity of different enthusiasms; a variety of style corresponding to the variety of artists . . .' Having so many of these qualifications himself, Diderot soon responded to what Bernard Berenson would have called the 'life-enhancing' properties of Chardin's work. While we examine one of the still-lives Diderot praised, the human condition, otherwise often so tedious and burdensome, seems a privilege we feel glad and proud to share. He irradiates every object he sees. 'There is nothing in nature', wrote the Goncourts, 'that his art cannot respect'. He enters the field, Proust would add, as authoritatively 'as does the light, giving its colour to everything, conjuring up from the timeless obscurity where they lay entombed all nature's creatures, animate or inanimate, together with the meaning of her design', a meaning that art alone can momentarily reveal.

* See *Marcel Proust on Art and Literature, 1896–1919*, translated by Sylvia Townsend Warner, 1984.

Like Rembrandt's, Chardin's self-portrait depicts the artist as a magnificent survivor.

Take a single canvas, entitled *Panier de Fraises des Bois*. Beside a glowing pyramid of wild strawberries, symmetrically piled up in a wicker basket, a couple of white carnations lie near the basket's edge, next to a solid tumbler full of white wine. The artist was never a moralist; he is merely representing the objects he has arranged upon his own domestic table-cloth; yet he manages to invest each separate detail of the composition with a deeply pleasurable significance – so long as there are strawberries growing in the woods, and there is wine to accompany a meal, we can hope to keep despair at bay. Chardin remained primarily a well-known painter of still-lives until the year 1753, when he exhibited a full-length portrait; and thenceforward he became more and more preoccupied with the human figure and with the comings and goings of an ordinary Parisian household. He painted children, whom he clearly loved – a little girl playing with a shuttlecock, a boy building a card-castle or talking to his mother on his way to school. He also depicted older members of the family – for example, a handsome servant-girl, *La Pourvoïeuse*, who just visited a local market, and *L'Oeconome*, an aged housekeeper in a frilled cap placidly doing her accounts.

Unlike Greuze, born a quarter of a century later, Chardin does not preach virtue or hint that the ordinary men and women he represents, because they are prosaic and unaffected, have any special claim to be admired. They are merely themselves, the kind of sober middle-class people among whom he had been brought up; and today the society to which Chardin belonged, the *bourgeoisie* of eighteenth-century France, seems to have occupied a peculiarly enviable position. Whatever might happen or be beginning to happen at a higher or a lower level, the skilled craftsman and the industrious tradesman then shared singularly well-ordered lives. They had their own *douceur de vivre*, which depended among other things, as Chardin's pictures of the dinner-table and the kitchen repeatedly show, upon the important art of cookery; and an authoritative manual *La Cuisinière Bourgeoise*, the earliest French recipe-book, appeared in 1746, when Chardin was forty-seven, and the Revolution, which would demolish both the bourgeois and the aristocratic 'sweetness of life', still lay many years ahead.

Chardin's self-portrait, executed during his old age, like Rembrandt's

masterpiece at Kenwood House, shows the artist as a magnificent survivor. Since above all else he cherished the gift of seeing, he wears a broad shade to protect his eyes, and balanced across his blunt nose a pair of big spectacles, while a nightcap warmly encompasses his head and a scarf is knotted round his neck. Few more unpretentious self-portraits have been painted by a great master. Chardin neither pretends he is an ordinary man, nor asserts he is a hero. The artist, he had once said, 'who has never felt the difficulty of art', would achieve nothing of any real value; and here he faces a complex yet fascinating task, which, thanks to a lifetime's hard practice, he does not for a moment doubt he will ultimately overcome. He records his physical appearance, and, doing so, his sense of his own identity, with the same imaginative skill that he has already devoted to his usual range of subjects – a basketful of strawberries, a glass of wine, a gleaming black bottle, an old kitchen-knife on a wrinkled sheet of newspaper, or a crumbling loaf of bread.

7

'Happy Living Things'

SAINT-EVREMOND, the elderly French exile whom Charles II had protected and befriended, was an Epicurean philosopher of the gentlest, most persuasive kind. He held many views on the human condition which he imparted with style and wit; and he maintained, for example, that, once a man had reached old age, nothing strengthened and supported life quite so happily as Love. Descartes' proposition, that we know we exist because we think, he considered much 'too cold and languishing'; it is because we retain the ability to fall in love, he said, that we are aware of being still alive. The fact that he himself was almost always enamoured – usually of a famous beauty, often far beyond his reach – 'sometimes bribes my imagination to suppose that I am young'.

He had other original opinions on how we should conduct our later years. 'When we grow old', he wrote, 'and our own spirits decay', to keep a number of living creatures about us 'and be much with them', has a delightfully restorative effect. Once Charles appointed him 'Keeper of the Ducks in the Decoy in St. James's Park', he could put this theory into practice. His London house was full of birds and beasts; and, unless he were at Whitehall, amusing the King or joking and roistering among rakish courtiers, they appear to have been his favourite companions. Saint-Evremond, of course, was not alone in his belief that the proximity of vigorous, attractive animals makes for human health and happiness, and that between animals and civilised man there is a very close connection, which has existed, archaeologists assure us, since the passing of the Ice Age. It was through this relationship that imaginative art first entered Europe. The Palaeolithic artist had learned to depict the beasts he hunted

[93]

long before he could produce equally convincing representations of the other members of his tribe; and, in the newly discovered Lascaux Cave, the only huntsman portrayed, a doomed figure lying near a ferocious bison's hooves, is a coarse and rudimentary sketch.

I was lucky enough to be able to visit the cave before ordinary sight-seers had been shut out; and I found the experience strangely moving, yet often curiously puzzling. Compared with many caves in the same region, it is neither long nor very wide, a passage that runs for some thirty metres into the flank of a small rocky hill; and its roof is both rather low and fantastically irregular. Over that crude surface sprawl the huge images, usually deer, wild oxen and small shaggy horses, black or a rich reddish brown, that the Palaeolithic artist left behind him. They have a wonderful verisimilitude – especially the great cattle that forever rear and gallop just above our heads; but, beside delighting, they also baffle and bewilder us, so difficult is it to understand either the creator's purpose or the technical methods he employed. Clearly he had little sense of order; one image may be superimposed upon the next. It never forms part of a general scene, but was evidently painted for its own sake, while the vivid impression it records was still vivid in the artist's memory.

The Palaeolithic painter seems to have been literally an impressionist. He fixed his immediate recollections of what he saw, and rendered the shape and density and weight of his subject with the help of an embracing outline, that conveys not only an animal's form but its essential character and movement. Although there are a few striking exceptions such as the so-called 'sorcerers', who appear to be masked magicians, and vague erotic female shapes, the human species seldom emerges on a painted cave-wall; and, if it does, like the dying huntsman at Lascaux, it is represented in a series of schematic strokes which embody not the artist's real vision but his childish conception of how a human body ought to be depicted. That primitive sketch (which archaeologists, for obvious reasons, call the 'Phallic Man') sets us a multitude of interesting problems. Why was he painted, between a bison and a rhinoceros, deep in a natural crevice or 'oubliette', his bird-headed staff, conjecturally a staff of office or a spear-thrower, which he seems to have dropped or flung down, lying at his right-hand side? It is thought by students of early cultures that he may perhaps have been a shaman, a prophet and priest, who, among his other gifts, understood the language of the animals. It is even suggested that his

antagonist, the ferocious wounded bison, was possibly a rival shaman in disguise.

Modern authorities are now inclined to agree that these prehistoric refuges – more than a hundred caves are known today – were once the scene of secret magic rites, and that their decorations gave huntsmen a mysterious power over the animals they hunted. A modern art-historian, however, the late Kenneth Clark, has advanced a very different view. In cave-paintings, he reminds us, men, compared with their prey, habitually 'cut very poor figures'; for animals, distinguished by their greater strength and speed, were at that time still in the ascendant, and men a wandering predatory species. 'Can we seriously believe', the historian asks, 'that they thought they were gaining power over their magnificent companions? Are they not rather expressing their envy and admiration? . . . Personally I believe that the animals in the cave paintings are records of admiration. "This is what we want to be like", they say, in unmistakable accents; "these are the most admirable of our kinsmen" . . .'*

Although Kenneth Clark, a peculiarly sophisticated writer, was perhaps not very well qualified to grasp the mentality of an unknown semi-savage people, it is an interesting hypothesis; and there seems no doubt that the Palaeolithic artist, to judge from the extraordinary sensitiveness with which he represented their grace and strength and decorative splendour, revered the animals on whom his life depended, and, now and then, felt for them a kind of love. At the same time, as an artist, he must certainly have *enjoyed* his work and, whatever his magic purposes may have been, experienced the special form of happiness that rewards creative effort.

Otherwise, it was a grim and dangerous world. During the Palaeolithic Age, a drab tundra stretched northwards across Europe as far as the glaciers of the ice-cap; and through that dismal landscape men dogged the itinerant herds, sometimes meeting their match in a rhinoceros or a mammoth, whose round baldish head, thick hairy coat and small fierce eyes above enormous curving tusks, often appears among the larger beasts they painted. During their long expeditions, their empty homes were frequently occupied by cave-bears, which have left piles of now fossilised droppings, scattered bones, claw marks, and, if the inner passages of the cave are particularly narrow, the traces of their shoulders on the rocks they

* *Animals and Man*, 1977.

[95]

Christ and his disciples at Emmaus by Paolo Veronese. Before them the master's children are playing with a noble dog.

rubbed smooth while they lumbered to and fro; and, once a tribe returned, the intruders, which presumably put up a savage resistance, had to be driven out again.

Into this harsh life came creative art and emotions we recognise and share today. The little museum at Altamira, the famous Spanish cave archaeologists first studied,* is one of the sacred places of European art-history; for there we are shown not only the lamps with which the Palaeolithic artists worked, almost always far from daylight, but the fresh-

* It was the Abbé Breuil who, at the beginning of the present century, first made careful drawings of its decorations. At times, however, he was apt to improve on, or over-elaborate, the images he sought to copy.

water shells they used as palettes and small heaps of the primitive substances that they employed as colours.

Once *homo sapiens*, now more and more master of his surroundings, had begun to domesticate and breed animals, a new chapter opened in the relationship of men and beasts, which art again reflected, and which at length found its way into literature, until it presently became a subject that concerned both philosophers and theologians. With Descartes' harsh assertion that an animal was a mere soulless piece of sentient machinery few poets and artists have agreed. In the works of most Renaissance painters, particularly in those of Paolo Veronese, huge handsome dogs sleeping, alertly reclining, being caressed by their master's children, occupy an honoured place; while the European 'Great Horse',* the breed that soldiers and sovereigns rode before the introduction of an Arab line, was admired and lovingly depicted.

At the Emperor's Viennese court, good horsemanship was an especially valued gift; and in 1574 two distinguished English visitors, Edward Wotton and the soldier-poet Sir Philip Sidney, often attended the Imperial riding-school, where they set themselves to learn the latest modes. Their instructor Ion Pietro Pugliano, Sidney writes, not only spoke admiringly of practised horsemen – 'the noblest of soldiers ... the maisters of war, and ornaments of peace, speedie goers, and strong abiders, triumphers both in Camps and Courts' – but eulogised the horse's nature, 'telling what a peerless beast the horse was . . . the beast of most bewtie, faithfulness, courage and much more, that if I had not been a peece of a Logician. . . . I think he would have persuaded mee to have wished myselfe a horse.'†

Thus the rough little horses that Palaeolithic man had chased and killed, frequently by driving a whole herd over a cliff, at length developed, some enthusiasts maintained, into counterparts of human virtue, just as the minor carnivores that must have slunk and scurried, until they were driven away, around pre-historic camp-fires, gradually established their privi-

---

* A fine specimen of the Great Horse is to be seen in the equestrian statue of Charles I that looks down London's Whitehall. The King, not every passer-by may have noticed, is mounted on a massive stallion.

† *Defence of Poesie*, Chapter I. For drawing my attention to this passage, I am indebted to my friend Patrick Leigh Fermor, himself an enthusiastic horseman, in his admirable travel-book *A Time of Gifts*, 1977.

leged positions in the households of mankind, and, among the ancient Egyptians, were identified with the powerful goddess Bast, 'the Lady of Life', who had a majestic feline head. Of all the animals that have accompanied the human race down the millennia, cats, thanks to their instinctive genius for survival, their blend of courage and strength and cunning, and to the beauty that, if they are well-loved and well-tended, almost every one of them possesses, have made a particularly strong appeal to the literary imagination; and some, through their portraits in literature and art, have now become historic characters – for instance, Montaigne's cat, of whom he wrote that, should they play together, he was never quite sure if he were playing with her, or she had decided she would play with him; the big black-and-white animal who sits protectively behind Shakespeare's friend Lord Southampton in a contemporary canvas painted at the Tower of London during his imprisonment; Horace Walpole's favourite, 'the pensive Selima', whose narcissistic death, 'Drowned in a Tub of Gold Fishes', was celebrated by Thomas Gray;* and Johnson's no less memorable 'Hodge', whom he fed on oysters he bought in Fleet Street, and Boswell watched scrambling up the great man's breast, 'while my friend smiling and half-whistling, rubbed down his back and pulled him by the tail; and when I observed he was a fine cat, saying, "Oh, yes, Sir, but I have had cats whom I liked better than this", and then as if perceiving Hodge to be out of countenance, adding, "but he is a very fine cat, a very fine cat indeed." '

Since the Cheshire Cat, from the branch of a tree in Wonderland, explained to Alice how little cats resembled dogs, their varying merits and demerits have been endlessly debated. Of dogs Anatole France once said that 'the dog knows reverence and knows shame – the cat knows neither; the dog has the elements of religion in him'; and it is certainly true that, although cats sometimes look furtive and apprehensive, they very seldom look guilty. Whereas we like and esteem dogs because we think they share some

* The beautiful line, in which Gray describes Selima while she gazes admiringly at her own reflection before she notices the goldfish, 'her conscious tail her joy declared', has often reminded me of a sentence of Beatrix Potter's *Tale of Peter Rabbit*: 'A white cat was staring at some gold fish. She sat very, very still, but now and then the tip of her tail twitched as if it were alive.'

of our virtues – and, probably, our sense of sin – for cats, besides admiring their natural grace, we feel an involuntary regard because, staunch amoralists that they are, they seem to have escaped so many of our human foibles. Here the contrasted behaviour of slumbering cats and dogs is particularly significant. Dogs and their masters are often equally anxious; a dog's anxieties pursue him into his dreams, and from his basket he stirs and sighs and growls,* while a cat, tired out by the day's adventures, which may have included hazardous thefts, desperate escapes and sanguinary crimes, appears to drop at once into a bottomless oblivion, the 'rêve sans fin' which Baudelaire admired.†

It is understandable that, in the nineteenth century, cats should have particularly delighted French Romantic painters and poets, and that both Delacroix and his ill-fated friend Géricault were devoted cat-observers. Each artist portrayed his subjects, just as Delacroix depicted lions at the Jardin des Plantes, from an essentially Romantic point of view – not as man's placid fireside-companions, but as patrician individualists. On a page of ten sketches of a single cat by Géricault, in each portrait he has caught a deep yawn or an impatient snarl; and Delacroix, who is said to have resembled a cat himself with his 'tawny feline eyes and thick arched brows', attempted to portray, above all else, his subjects' air of untamed pride. Contemporary poets and prose-writers followed Delacroix's example. Baudelaire, apostle of literary dandyism and arch-opponent of bourgeois standards, suggests in *Fusées*, his posthumously published notebook, that cats are patrician dandies of the animal world; and that it is easy enough to understand why modern democrats detest them: 'the cat is good-looking; he reveals ideas of luxury, cleanliness, physical pleasure'. Three poems concerned with the beauty and pagan hardihood of cats are included in *Les Fleurs du Mal*; while Théophile Gautier, to whom the poet dedicated *Les Fleurs*, had a cat called Éponine.‡ Although she frequently leant against his writing-arm, he would encourage her to share his desk, and, as a further mark of his esteem, allotted her a regular place at his domestic dinner-table.

---

* 'Like a dog, he hunts in dreams': Tennyson, *Locksley Hall*.

† '*Ils prennent en songeant les nobles attitudes Des grands sphinx allongés au fond des solitudes Qui semblent s'endormir dans un rêve sans fin . . .*'

‡ See *La Nature chez elle, et Ménagerie Intime*. Éponine, after whom Gautier named his cat, was a heroine of Gallo-Roman history.

The head of a cat by Delacroix.

According to Kenneth Clark in a passage I have quoted above, the earliest artists may have felt both admiration and a touch of deep envy for the beasts they and their tribe hunted; and that mixture of feelings still emerges, now and then, in the work of modern writers. It is not so much their relationship with, as their dissimilarity from ourselves, that helps to give most animals their fascination; and for Walt Whitman, at least, it also manifested their considerable superiority. This was the reason, he declared in *Leaves of Grass*, that he sometimes wished to live with them:

'. . . They are so placid and self-contained . . .
They do not sweat and whine about their condition,
They do not lie awake in the dark and weep for their sins,
They do not make me sick discussing their duty to God . . .
Not one is respectable or industrious over the whole earth.'

Another distinguishing trait that all animals possess, and that constantly excites our envy, is their freedom from the rule of Time. Unaffected by the dreadful procession of Yesterday, Today and Tomorrow, they exist in an Eternal Present. Thoughts of the past bring them no regrets and ideas of the future no alarm. One of the most moving passages in the *Odyssey* relates how the hero, while re-entering his island kingdom heavily disguised, had passed his old hound Argos, whom he himself had bred, but who, neglected and 'full of vermin', lay abandoned on a dung-heap; and how Argos, suddenly aware of his master's presence, 'wagged his tail and dropped both his ears', though nearer to Odysseus 'he lacked the strength to move'. Yet, after all, despite this sudden flash of memory, I doubt if poor Argos really 'remembered' Odysseus or his own vigorous youth in the accepted meaning of the word. Had he been a deserted human servitor, his fate might have been much more poignant; during their long separation he would then have been repeatedly thinking of his loss, and of the carefree days when the huntsmen 'used to lead him out against wild goats and deer and hares'. But for Homer's Argos, despite his vanished happiness and his wretched old age, the past was as vague and insubstantial as a dream. Nor did he suspect that, now he had again caught sight of Odysseus, 'black death' would very soon descend. Man, wrote André Malraux, is the only species of animal that knows it is bound presently to die.

Whether animals possess 'souls' and, if that be true, whether in some form they may conceivably enter Heaven, is a problem that has often troubled Christian thinkers. Marlowe's Dr Faustus, facing the dread result of his compact with the Devil, exclaims in his agony that he would willingly accept a subordinate form of life to escape unending retribution:

A cat in different moods; ten sketches by Géricault.

> '. . . all beasts are happy,
> For when they die,
> Their souls are soon dissolv'd in elements'

They lose, that is to say, their separate identity and vanish into the great flood of terrestrial existence. A modern theologian, on the other hand, C. S. Lewis, author of *The Problem of Pain*, found it 'difficult to suppose that the apes, the elephants and the higher domestic animals, have not, in some degree, a self or soul' which might possibly survive death, and observes that, although the Fathers of the Church held the opposite view, so far as he is concerned a Heaven completely stripped of beasts would be a much less paradisial place.

Today from some regions of the earth, for example, from the cities of modern China, dogs, we learn, have been ruthlessly removed. But such a deprivation even a Communist government would not venture to impose on the citizens of any Western state; our relationship with and affection for animals is now too deeply engrained in our ways of life and thought. When Saint-Evremond recommended that, particularly during our old age, we should surround ourselves with other living creatures, he was already addressing the converted. Robert Herrick kept an intelligent pig, which he had taught to use a tankard; at Whitehall, Charles II shared his bedchamber with the spaniels that bore his name; and the household of a seventeenth-century country gentleman – unlike Saint-Evremond no philosopher, but evidently a shrewd manager of his own existence, since, we are told, he 'lived to a hundred, never lost his eyesight but always writ and read without spectacles and got to horse without help' – is admirably described in an autobiographical fragment written by the first Lord Shaftesbury, 'the false *Achitophel*' of Dryden's satire:

'Mr. Hastings . . . was peradventure an original in our age, or rather the copy of our nobility in ancient times . . . His house was perfectly of the old fashion, in the midst of a large park well stocked with deer . . . The parlour was a large long room . . . On a great hearth paved with brick lay some terriers and the choicest hounds and spaniels; seldom but two of the great chairs had litters of young cats in them, which were not to be disturbed, he having always three or four attending him at dinner, and a little white stick of fourteen inches long lying by his trencher that he might defend such meat as he had no mind to part with to them.'

During the next century, though cats may no longer have fed from a gentleman's own plate, the presence of animals was held to confer both physical and psychological advantages. Regularly inhaled, the wholesome breath of a cow, it was supposed, might often cure tuberculosis; and a well-known specialist had opened a private hospital where a partition, conveniently placed behind the bed, would every night be drawn up to bring the patient into easy breathing-distance of a milch-cow ruminating in her stall. Her proximity, the physician believed, would effect a natural cure; for, the Romantic Age having then dawned, Nature was regarded as a fount of health and wisdom; and it was a great Romantic poet, Samuel Taylor Coleridge, who described how the sight of happy and beautiful creatures, playing in their native element, had enabled an unhappy, guilt-obsessed man to at last throw off his load.

The original version of *The Rime of the Ancient Mariner* was composed in 1797, a year after Coleridge, 'the rapt One, of the godlike forehead', having leapt over their orchard fence, first appeared upon the Wordworths' threshold, and been quickly recognised by William as the 'only wonderful man' that he had ever known. But Coleridge's senescence began early. Although many years would pass before the young visionary, who dazzled the Wordsworths, became 'the fat, flabby, incurvated personage' whose prophetic voice had 'contracted itself into a plaintive snuffle and singsong', while, pontificating about some philosophic subject, he zigzagged down a garden walk,* his hopes had very soon declined. 'The poet is dead in me', he declared in 1801; and he gradually acquired a load of guilt that an unsuccessful marriage and his frustrated love for Sarah Hutchinson were perpetually increasing. Yet, as sometimes happens, Coleridge's sense of guilt seems to have attacked him before it had a genuine cause. He was twenty-five, and still a poetic enthusiast, when he wrote the *Ancient Mariner*. Yet his theme was already guilt and remorse; they provide the burden that the grim old protagonist carries slung around his shoulders.

Taken as a whole, Coleridge's poetic narrative is an odd, uneven work. The Mariner himself, distinguished by his 'glittering eye' and the clutching hand he employs to buttonhole the unfortunate Wedding Guest, at least until he starts to tell his tremendous tale is the self-centred Neurotic

* Carlyle: *Reminiscences: Edward Irving.*

and, indeed, the Social Bore personified; and Coleridge, where he blends the 'sublime' and the 'horrid', seems to have borrowed some of the paraphernalia of the late-eighteenth-century 'Gothick' novel. Yet again and again his imaginative genius appears. The peace that he rarely achieved through ratiocination he often reached through observation. He was an exquisite observer; and his notebooks contain numerous vivid records of the natural phenomena that enchanted him – the behaviour of birds, the ascension of sun and moon, the noise of the wind, phosphorescent surges sweeping beside a ship, and, twice affectionately described, a fountain on the sea-shore: 'The spring with the tiny little cone of loose sand ever rising and sinking at the bottom, but its surface without a wrinkle'; and, elsewhere, 'a fountain with unwrinkled surface yet still the living motion at the bottom, that "with soft and even pulse" keeps it full.'

Just as Coleridge's observations of the natural world helped to ease his moral sufferings, and brought him a happiness he could find neither in his philosophic musings nor in his practical experience of life, so the Ancient Mariner, when from his becalmed ship he notices the beauty of the water-snakes, creatures far freer and immeasurably less thought-burdened than himself, circling around its sides, suddenly discards his burden; and the dead albatross, symbol of his own guilt, sinks 'like lead into the sea':

> 'Beyond the shadow of the ship,
> I watch'd the water-snakes:
> They moved in tracks of shining white,
> And when they rear'd, the elfish light
> Fell off in hoary flakes.
>
> Within the shadow of the ship
> I watch'd their rich attire:
> Blue, glossy green, and velvet black,
> They coil'd and swam; and every track
> Was a flash of golden fire.
>
> O happy living things! no tongue
> Their beauty might declare:
> A spring of love gush'd from my heart,
> And I bless'd them unaware:

Sure my kind saint took pity on me,
And I bless'd them unaware.'

Thus, although the grace of animals and their presence around us, as Saint-Evremond said, may be a concomitant of happiness, merely because we relate them to our own life, and we sometimes think they share our feelings, their essential difference – few creatures could be more remote from humanity than an oceanic water-snake – is almost equally appealing. 'How do you know,' demanded Blake in his early masterpiece *The Marriage of Heaven and Hell*, 'but ev'ry Bird that cuts the airy way, is an immense world of delight, clos'd by your senses five?' 'Energy', he added, 'is Eternal Delight'; 'every thing that lives is Holy'. Thus the small signs that mark the passage of an unseen animal may themselves acquire a mysterious significance – for example, the strange labyrinth of silvery interwoven tracks left by a predatory snail over a single slab of garden-pavement. Where the snail hides, and why its search for food is so extraordinarily circuitous, are puzzles I have never solved. Yet, morning after morning, it has inscribed a similarly complex design, which resembles the calligraphic scribblings of an accomplished modern draughtsman, before it crawls home into its secret crevice; and each day, when I open the garden-door, I am happy to observe its latest work, and wish that I could follow the designer's plan.

8

'La Chasse au Bonheur'

IT is difficult nowadays to reread the Emperor Napoleon's biography without an occasional pang of horror; in almost every episode, the personality he shows the world seems to become more and more repellent. Thus, during the first furies of the Revolution, we meet him as an ambitious young officer who, at the siege of Toulon, had told Barras that a true patriot could not be 'revolutionary enough', but, watching a Parisian mob invade the Tuileries, quickly drops into coarse Italian slang: '*Che Coglione*', he exclaims, 'they should have swept away four or five hundred with cannon, and the rest would still be running'. Then we move on to one of his greatest campaigns, to Eylau, where in February 1807 he vanquished both the Russian and the Prussian armies, and twenty-nine thousand dead are lying scattered. While he strides across the field, followed by his brilliant troop of Marshals, he pauses to turn over one or two corpses with his boot, remarking dispassionately 'small change!'* The expression was characteristic; Napoleon often spoke of his ability to 'afford' soldiers, and 'replace' them if a temporary reverse occurred. His fellow men were merely an array of ciphers on his prodigious balance-sheet.

Yet, despite the demonic military genius he revealed at the height of his powers, even in those days his private character appears sometimes to have been curiously crude and commonplace. Notwithstanding the air of imperial grandeur that he presently assumed, he had little natural distinction. He retained, said Jean-Antoine Chaptal, Minister of the Interior during the Consulate, 'the manners of an ill-bred young

* See Jean Savant: *Napoléon raconté par les témoins de sa vie*, 1954.

[107]

lieutenant', and no one, at a rapid glance, would have thought that he possessed 'the smallest knowledge of society'. As the First Consul, if he were receiving guests, he might 'come out of his study whistling, accost women without breaking off . . . and go back again humming an Italian song'. Towards women, indeed, his behaviour was usually brusque and now and then strangely brutal. Neither in conversation, nor in his random love affairs, did he ever spare their feelings; 'he would have liked', wrote Madame de Rémusat, the Empress Josephine's aristocratic confidante and *dame du palais*, 'to be the sole master of reputations, and make and unmake them at pleasure. He would compromise a man or tarnish a woman for a word . . .'

That a strain of native brutality ran through his character his former school-friend Louis de Bourrienne noted. Should he be opposed or, for any other reason, particularly annoyed, he would sit down behind his desk, tilt his chair back at a dangerous angle, and vent his exasperation on the chair's right arm, mutilating the wood with a penknife that he carried for that special purpose. Napoleon seems very seldom to have regretted the past, or doubted the rightness of his own actions. During his exile, questioned by a devoted follower about the judicial assassination of the gallant young duc d'Enghien, the House of Condé's last heir, he accepted complete responsibility for the crime – it was less a crime than a terrible mistake, Talleyrand subsequently observed – and spoke of the victim's kidnapping and execution as a necessary dynastic *coup*. Why, he asked, had the subject been brought up? 'The Enghien affair? Pooh! What is one man, after all?'

His cynicism, however, was half his political strength. Great fame, such as he possessed, he once explained to Bourrienne, was primarily 'a great noise. The more one makes the further it carries. Laws, institutions, monuments, nations, all have their day. But noise remains, and resounds in other ages'. This was a topic to which he frequently reverted; 'my power derives from my glory', he told his intimates, 'and would collapse if I failed to base it on more glory and fresh victories . . . Conquest alone can maintain me'. Napoleon, Bourrienne believed, was 'not disposed by temperament to think well of mankind'; there were two great levers, he asserted, capable of moving men, 'fear and interest'. Affection he had always discounted; 'friendship is only a word', his old friend heard him say, adding that himself he 'cared for nobody'.

Yet his voice and the echo of his victorious achievements carried wonderfully well, and easily traversed frontiers. In England he soon acquired, and long retained, many enthusiastic advocates, among whom Byron was one of the most eloquent. News of the Emperor's abdication, at Fontainebleau on April 20th, 1814, struck the poet with the force of a personal blow. He had just left his beloved sister in the country, and 'on my return [he wrote] found my poor little pagod, Napoleon, pushed off his pedestal; – the thieves are in Paris', the thieves, of course, being the Bourbon dynasty and their foreign supporters, who championed 'the dull, stupid old system – balance of Europe – poising straws upon kings' noses . . .'. Meanwhile, he had composed 'a very beautiful *Ode to Napoleon Buonaparte*'; and in 1815, at the end of the Hundred Days, when he heard that the Emperor had fought his last battle and was rapidly falling back towards Paris, Byron declared that he felt 'damned sorry for it', adding after a pause, 'I didn't know but I might live to see Lord Castlereagh's head on a pole. But I shan't, now'.

Later, we hear, he had sought the first refusal of Napoleon's Coronation robes, which a London tradesman had acquired and hoped to sell; and, as he prepared to bid England goodbye, he commissioned a magnificent new travelling carriage, 'copied from the celebrated one of Napoleon taken at Genappe'. That the poet to some extent identified himself with the Emperor, at least during his more hubristic moments, is shown by an account of his 'fractious' moods and wild remarks that Augusta Leigh sent in 1816 to the 'unforgiving' wife, who had just deserted him. He regarded himself, he had then proclaimed, as 'the greatest man' alive; and when his cousin, Captain George Byron, who happened also to be present, put in tentatively 'Except Bonaparte?', hoping maybe that he could give his conversation a slightly less vainglorious turn, 'God, I don't know that I do except even him,' Byron immediately replied.

Had a confrontation between the poet and the emperor ever taken place, it would have formed a fascinating addition to the narratives of Napoleon's interviews with Chateaubriand and Goethe, but, like those occasions, perhaps, have had very few results. Napoleon was not at home in the company of writers, and took little genuine interest in books, or in the arts generally, unless they served some political purpose, as Chateaubriand's

Génie du Christianisme had done, or enhanced his own imperial renown. Ossian, the fictitious Gaelic bard, invented by James Macpherson about the middle of the eighteenth century, whose verses celebrated the deeds of heroic antique warriors, remained Napoleon's favourite poet; while, again according to Chaptal, 'having been informed that David was the first painter of the day', he repeated this view, but did not venture into any detailed comparisons with other distinguished modern artists. On the merits of Greek and Roman literature, he held typically strong opinions, revered Homer but mistrusted Virgil, believed that Suetonius, since he had described the crimes committed by the early Roman emperors, was 'the worst historian of antiquity', and that Horace's *Odes* were 'only fit for sybarites'. In seventeenth- and eighteenth-century French literature, he detested Racine, Voltaire and Rousseau, but had a due respect for Corneille, whose tributes to the value of 'duty' and 'honour' struck a much more useful note.

Yet Napoleon's influence, or, rather the influence of his tremendous career, on nineteenth-century Romantic writers, their conception of life and their quest of individual happiness, was extraordinarily far-reaching. Poets and novelists, who might have been expected to revolt against his cruel record, were carried away by his legendary appeal; and a young German poet, Heinrich Heine, in his imaginative discursion *Reisebilder*, would draw a particularly flattering portrait of the victorious dynast at his ease. The background was Dusseldorf's Court Garden:

> 'The Emperor with his attendants rode directly down the avenue . . . He wore his invisible-green uniform and the little world-renowned hat. He rode a white steed . . . Calmly, almost lazily, sat the Emperor, holding his rein with one hand, and with the other good-naturedly patting the horse's neck. It was a sunny marble hand, a mighty hand . . . Even the face had that hue which we find in the marble of Greek and Roman busts; the traits were as nobly cut as in the antique . . . Those lips smiled . . . It was an eye as clear as Heaven . . .'

Later, it is true, still an unknown young man 'of student-like appearance', Heine returned to Dusseldorf and, sitting in the same garden,

watched French prisoners of war, captured during the retreat from Moscow, now tattered and miserable, slowly trudging home. Yet his vision of the divinised despot somehow never quite faded; and two great French novelists, Stendhal and Balzac, who also cherished it, continued to revere his memory. Since, under Napoleon's influence, they invented and put into action a new mode of seeking happiness, their readers will certainly ask if the Emperor himself expressed any views upon the subject. But again his opinions appear to have been fairly commonplace. Talking about happiness with an intelligent young woman, Victoire de Chastenay, one day in 1795, 'he said that for a man it must lie in the greatest possible development of his faculties';* and his companion, who did not then know that he had merely quoted the eighteenth-century philosopher Condillac, author of *Traité des sensations*, thought that the remark was 'dazzling'.

At the time, his triumphs had scarcely begun. But, towards the end, on the eve of his abdication, he came to believe, like Saint-Just, that his true aim had been primarily to improve the condition of his fellow citizens. 'I have meant to make France happy', he assured his generals gathered around him at Fontainebleau; 'I have not succeeded. Events have turned against me.' Finally, on St. Helena, he spoke of the dream he had always hoped he might realise. He had looked forward to a happy old age when he would drive around his peaceful Empire, accompanied by the Empress and their son, in an open carriage behind their own horses, visiting every corner of his dominions, 'receiving complaints, redressing wrongs, and scattering public buildings and benefactions wherever we went'.

Far less prosaic were the aspirations of the two novelists on whose life and works he made so strong a mark. They envisaged Napoleon as an irresistible conqueror rather than as a disappointed benefactor. Balzac's guests in 1828, besides admiring his elegant roseate bathroom and his resplendent bedroom (which resembled the 'bridal chamber of a fifteen-year-old duchess') when they examined his magnificent study, saw among red morocco-bound volumes stamped with his fictitious ancestral arms, a plaster statuette of the Emperor and, attached to its scabbard, a grandiloquent inscription that the novelist had signed: '*What he could not achieve by the sword I shall accomplish by the pen*'. Henri Beyle, who, for reasons unknown, adopted the pseudonym Stendhal after an obscure middle-

* Jean Savant, op. cit.

[111]

Honoré de Balzac; a photograph by Félix Nadar. A great
admirer of Napoleon, 'what the Emperor could not achieve
by the sword', he proclaimed, 'he would accomplish by
the pen'.

European town, was equally devoted to the Napoleonic legend; and in 1821 he wrote his own epitaph, where he enumerated his great aesthetic passions – Cimarosa, Shakespeare, Mozart, Coreggio – listed the initials of the women he had passionately loved, four or five of whom, he thought, had loved him – and informed posterity that the Emperor Napoleon was 'the only man he had respected'. Nor did he change his view; at the end of his life he would sit at the fireside of his old Spanish friend the comtesse de Montijo, and recount the glorious exploits of the *Grande Armée* to her appreciative daughters, one of whom, the beautiful Eugénie, would presently become the Empress of the French.

Stendhal's cult seems all the more remarkable since he had himself been engaged in Napoleon's most disastrous campaign, had witnessed the occupation of Moscow and the terrible retreat that followed. From the Emperor's example both he and Balzac had inherited a dominant idea. Happiness, they believed, was not a fortuitous gift – and certainly not the reward of moral virtue – which we should patiently await, but a benefit we must pursue and conquer by the bold exercise of skill and energy. '*La chasse au bonheur*' preoccupied them all their lives; and the pursuit is repeatedly portrayed, under realistic or symbolic forms, in the novels that they wrote. Balzac's version of what constituted real happiness was the more material of the two. As Proust objected in *Contre Sainte-Beuve*, his genius was counterbalanced by a 'vulgarity so massive that a lifetime could not leaven it'. His hero Rastignac, type of the fiercely determined young *arriviste*, sets before us as his goal 'the most grovelling ambitions'; while Balzac himself, having achieved the boldest of his romantic designs, and at last persuaded Madame Hanska, a rich and cultivated Polish noblewoman, to become his wife, wrote reminding his favourite sister Laure that, whatever she might think or say, in Paris it meant a great deal 'to throw open one's house and entertain the cream of society, who will meet a woman there who is polished, stately as a queen . . . related to the grandest families, witty, well-educated and handsome'.* Balzac's vision, once the marriage had taken place, almost immediately dissolved; he was then much too ill and tired to enjoy his matrimonial triumph; but it is clear that, having, with the *Comédie Humaine*, rounded off his gigantic literary campaign and drawn 'a

* *Marcel Proust on Art and Literature*, translated by Sylvia Townsend Warner, introduced by Terence Kilmartin, 1984.

complete picture of society from which nothing had been omitted', he expected to conquer the dominant social position he had always ardently desired.

By comparison, Beyle, although, as Stendhal, he dreamt of literary glory, set no great value on immediate public acclaim or on the social renown that might perhaps accompany it. For him '*La Chasse au Bonheur*' was a wholly private concern; he did not expect that the books in which he described the pursuit would immediately be welcomed, but liked to assume, he said, that his true qualities might be recognised about 1880, or possibly 1935, when he had gathered a sympathetic audience and could 'dine late' among 'the happy few'. Meantime, he coined the magic word '*Beylism*', to describe his own method of organising and executing his lifelong chase. Whether he listened to music, met friends he loved, revisited a city he had once admired, or surveyed a tremendous battle-scene, it consisted in arranging a pattern of recollections, emotions and ideas that gave him a sense of being vigorously and enjoyably alive. At the same time, he must be able to satisfy his insatiable appetite for knowledge.

Happiness, he had decided, was the product of 'love + work'. There is a strange resemblance, it has often struck me, between Henri Beyle and James Boswell. The latter's Swiss servant Jacob complained that 'Monsieur had not the habits of a gentleman'; he was too open-hearted and perpetually asking questions that his unfortunate domestic was obliged to answer; '*il voudrait savoir tout au fond*'. Beyle's interrogative attitude towards life is endlessly reflected by his novels, *Le Rouge et le Noir*, published in 1831, and *La Chartreuse de Parme*, the product of less than two months' work, which appeared in 1839, and Balzac then saluted as a 'masterpiece of the literature of ideas'. With the Romantic spirit, Beyle combined the enquiring scepticism of an eighteenth-century *philosophe*. Few things was he prepared to take for granted; he was perpetually investigating his protagonists' real motives, delving into their minds and seeking to discover the secret '*fond des choses*' beneath any given situation. What always most concered him were the different means his characters adopted during their individual search for happiness; and his chief aim was himself to see and write clearly. 'If I don't see clearly', he confessed, 'my whole world is totally destroyed'.

During at least one or two periods of his life, when *Beylism* brought him rich rewards, he must be regarded as a happy man – in Northern Italy, principally at Milan, a city for which he felt a keen affection,* where he had loved Angela Pietragrua, 'adored music and literary glory', and, being a Napoleonic dragoon, fought a duel and 'greatly esteemed the art of giving a good sabre-stroke'; and, more unexpectedly, over twenty years later, in London, a metropolis he otherwise detested. Between these two epochs he had had several vivid experiences of a less pacific kind as he followed Napoleon's advance across Europe, nearly witnessed the battle of Jena, seen the Emperor ride into Berlin and, on the heights of Bautzen, from the safety of a good open carriage, observed 'all the complex movements of an army of 140,000 men opposing another army of 160,000'.† Despite the tremendous cannonade, which might have distracted any other man, he calmly noted in his journal that it had been 'a splendid day for *Beylism*'.

At Moscow, too, in 1812, the Beylistic method had produced admirable results. 'As we left the city,' he recorded, its buildings were 'lit up by the loveliest conflagration in the world, forming an immense pyramid that was like the prayers of the faithful, the base on the earth and the apex in the heavens'. Although he escaped the worst horrors of the ensuing retreat, it cured him of all his military ambitions; he was glad to take refuge in the humdrum consular service, and at length settled down quietly and resignedly at Civitavecchia, a drab Italian sea-port town. Yet even there his pursuit of knowledge and the hunt for happiness continued; and it would scarcely slacken until his death in 1842. 'My own soul', he explained, 'is a fire that suffers if it does not blaze. I need three or four cubic feet of new ideas a day, as a steam-boat needs coal'; and the fuel he demanded he never ceased to provide, while he moved thoughtfully towards old age.

Of all his lesser-known works, his autobiographical *Souvenirs d'Égotisme*,‡ begun at Rome, during a holiday from Civitavecchia, in June 1832, is

---

* Here, in October 1816, Stendhal met and talked of the Emperor with Byron: '*un joli et charmant jeune homme*', he wrote, '. . . *c'est l'original de Lovelace* . . .'
† At this battle, as at Eylau on February 1807, Napoleon, in May 1813, defeated both the Russian and the Prussian forces.
‡ Long hidden away among Stendhal's unpublished writings, it first appeared in 1892, when it was warmly welcomed by the fashionable novelist, Paul Bourget. The present text, translated as *Memoirs of an Egoist* by T.W. Earp, came out in 1949.

probably the most revealing. Here, for example, he recounted a visit in
1821 to London, whither, 'profoundly disgusted with Parisian life', he had
gone 'to find a cure for the spleen'. His quest had 'succeeded well enough'.
But, although he much enjoyed watching Edmund Kean on the stage and
strolling beside the Thames 'towards *Little Chelsea*', whose small houses
'set off with rose-trees' he 'found truly elegiac' – it was the first time, he
adds, that he had been 'affected by the sentimental mode' – London, as a
rule, did not encourage his researches. His hotel, which overlooked
Covent Garden, seemed a strange and gloomy place; the bedroom he
occupied was ridiculously cramped; but he breakfasted off 'an infinity of
beefsteaks', in a gigantic dining-room; and every morning, down a broad
arcade, he watched 'about thirty good Englishmen, walking gravely, and
many of them looking unhappy'. Nor was he always very happy himself
until an odd adventure, slight but memorable, occurred to brighten his
existence.

In London he had certain French companions; and, while with one of
them, a friend named Barot, an intelligent banker from Lunéville, he was
discussing the laborious life of the English poor, and remarked that the
poor Italian was 'infinitely nearer to happiness' – at least, 'he has time to
make love' – Barot's foppish young English valet, who seemed to think
that 'his national honour was slighted', broke into their conversation.
Beyle having replied that if, as foreigners, they failed to appreciate
London, their failure might be due to the fact that they had no pleasant
feminine acquaintances, 'I'll manage that for you, sir', the valet helpfully
announced; and next day he told them of an assignation he had arranged
and a bargain he had struck. He had insisted, he said, that the gentlemen
should be given early-morning tea; and the girls in question finally agreed
to 'grant their good graces and their tea for twenty-one shillings'. They
inhabited, on the other hand, 'a lost quarter', called the Westminster Road;
and English acquaintances quickly pointed out that Beyle and Barot would
be 'taken miles away from London' and probably fall into an ambush, and
be beaten and robbed by a gang of ruffianly sailors.

Nevertheless, after some hesitation, the intrepid tourists decided to set
out, summoned a cab and, having twice or thrice been nearly overturned as
they passed through 'so-called streets without any pavement', were
deposited at the door of a three-storeyed house 'perhaps twenty-five feet
high', and received by 'three slender girls of small stature, with beautiful

chestnut hair, rather shy, very anxious to please, very pale'. Everything about the house into which Beyle and Barot were led was pathetically diminutive; 'the furniture seemed meant for dolls', and the visitors, being themselves fairly substantial, were afraid to sit down. 'Our little girls noticed our embarrassment; their own increased.' But then Barot, clearly a good-hearted man, thought of mentioning the garden. ' "Oh, we have a garden," they said, not boastfully, but with a kind of joy at having an object of luxury to show us.' The garden, which they explored by candle-light, was just as small as the house, extremely narrow and some twenty-five feet long; but it contained a laundry-tub and even a little vat for brewing beer. Barot laughed, and suggested that it was time to pay and go home. But Beyle objected that they must not hurt the girls' feelings.

Thus an occasion that, in other circumstances, might have been both sad and squalid, for the novelist acquired all the charm of a romantic fairy-tale. It was the girls' essential innocence, so different from the well-advertised virtue of such eighteenth-century heroines as Bernardin de Saint-Pierre's preposterous Virginie,* that at once touched his impressionable heart. Here, he felt, was native human goodness; and 'it seemed as though I was with tender friends whom I was seeing again after being a year away'. Both he and Barot had arrived with numerous defensive weapons; and when they went to bed, he was slightly alarmed by the discovery that none of the doors had either lock or key. But then, after all, he reflected, of what use would a locked door have been? A single blow of a man's fist would have demolished the flimsy brick partitions.

In bed, he was anxious to keep the light burning; but 'the modesty of my new friend, albeit so obedient and so good, would never consent. She made a gesture of obvious fear when I spread my pistols and daggers on the night-table . . . she was charming, small, well-made, pale. Nobody murdered us. The next morning we let them off their tea'; and when their hostesses heard that they proposed to spend the day in London – Barot was anxious to examine 'the brazen young women who then filled the foyer at Covent Garden' – but would very soon return, Beyle's bed-fellow, whose name, we learn, was Miss Appleby, declared that she wouldn't leave the

* In *Paul et Virginie* the heroine prefers death by drowning to making a gesture that would have saved her life, but might perhaps have looked immodest.

house if she could hope that he would certainly return that night. And so he did, having throughout the whole day 'only thought of a good, calm, quiet evening (*so snug!*)* that awaited me . . . What is amusing is that during my stay in England, I was unhappy when I could not finish my evenings at that house.'

Although the happiness Beyle found in the Westminster Road was scarcely a Napoleonic triumph, it was the 'first real and intimate consolation' he had experienced since he left Paris; and, in 1832, he clearly much enjoyed recording it. The story of his Lilliputian adventures, he thought, might serve an important literary purpose: 'If this book is boring, at the end of two years it will be wrapping up butter at the grocer's; if not, it will be seen that egotism, *so long as it is sincere*, is a means of depicting the human heart', in the knowledge of which he and his contemporaries, he thought, had recently 'made giants' strides . . .'.

When he slipped back into Parisian life, he felt stronger and far more self-confident. His memories of the great Emperor continued to inspire his efforts; but by 1832 the climate of the age had changed; for, once Napoleon had fallen, the young, whether, or not they had revered the Emperor themselves, suffered a pervasive sense of loss. France had ceased to be a country where juvenile talents were soon recognised, and might be wonderfully rewarded, where anything seemed possible, and, amid the announcement of victories and a beating of drums, marshals, dukes and princes were created overnight. What Byron had denounced as 'the dull, stupid old system' seemed once again to have descended on the world; and young men, now that they had lost the grand Napoleonic impetus, aspired towards much more spiritual but considerably vaguer goals. 'We were living at that time' wrote Gérard de Nerval in 1853, prefacing his poetic novel *Sylvie*, through 'one of those strange periods which usually follow a revolution or the downfall of some mighty empire . . . composed of activity, diffidence and inertia, splendid utopian dreams, philosophic or religious aspirations, hazy enthusiasms, the whole interpenetrated by certain instincts of renewal . . .'. But the young now lacked a sense of purpose, '*l'ambition n'était . . . pas de nôtre age*'; and, although the hunt for happiness continued, it had begun, during the 1830s, to take a much more visionary turn.

* Here the author, as he was fond of doing, uses an English phrase.

9

'The Valley of the Shadow'

WHEN Byron, in July 1823, embarked on his last voyage, he carried with him a variety of books, Scott's *Life of Swift*, Grimm's *Correspondence*, Colonel Hippesley's account of an expedition to South America, accompanied by the *Maximes* of François de la Rochefoucauld, a classic he already knew well; and, as the *Hercules* began its journey south, he preferred to sit alone and read. He 'looked unusually silent and serious', noted his travelling companion Edward Trelawny. He did not expect he would ever return from Greece, he had told the Blessingtons at Genoa; and in this mood he must have found the cool, sharp seventeenth-century aphorist, who had dismissed almost every pleasing illusion, but bidden his readers eschew humbug, cultivate self-knowledge, learn to understand and endure and see the world just as it is, a particularly sympathetic guide.

During past years, Byron had sometimes quoted from La Rochefoucauld, and once cursed him for 'being always right! In him a lie were virtue – or at least a comfort to his readers'; and, when he reopened the book, his eye would certainly have rested on the hundred-and-thirteenth maxim, where he reminds us that, although some marriages are perfectly tolerable, none is totally delectable – '*il y a de bons mariages, mais il n'y en a point de délicieux*'. Of La Rouchefoucauld's own marriage we know regrettably little, except that, at the age of fifteen, he had become the husband of a suitably well-born girl, Andrée de Vivonne, offspring of the Grand Falconer of France and, like Byron's wife, an heiress, who, before she died in 1670, had borne him numerous sons and daughters. Men of our class don't talk about our wives he had remarked; and we may therefore assume that Madame de la Rochefoucauld customarily stayed at home and was

content to do her matrimonial duty and await her husband's dashing visits, while, caught up in the two French civil wars, nicknamed *La Fronde*,* that raged between 1648 and 1653, he and his bellicose mistress, the duchesse de Longueville, galloped valiantly around France. By 1665, however, when his masterpiece first appeared, he was beginning to grow old and gouty, and had long ago settled down to enjoy his memories and reflections. Much of his time was now spent with some of the cleverest women in Paris, particularly with his close and dear friend – she may perhaps have been his last great love – Madame de Lafayette, authoress of *La Princesse de Clèves*. At her house, Madame de Sévigné describes him in April 1671 for her cherished daughter's benefit, as a favourite *ami de la maison*, making slightly unkind fun of another guest's far-too-girlish coiffure, which her hostess had just declared was '*complètement ridicule*', but which he gently affected to applaud: '*Ma mère, ah! par ma foi, mère*, we cannot stand for that. Come a little closer – *Ma mère*, you really look quite good.' Her daughter will 'recognise that tone', Madame de Sévigné comments.

I wish that some admirer could have overheard Byron's remarks on La Rochefoucauld's opinion of the married state. No doubt, they were violent, possibly rather scabrous; to him, even at the end of his career, his wife's 'unforgiving' behaviour was still a very painful subject. Few marriages have ended more suddenly and abruptly, or brought the partners less contentment. It was, indeed, almost the exact reverse of the kind of 'happy marriage' that, except for Thackeray in *Vanity Fair*, so many popular Victorian novelists would sketch upon their closing pages. At the time, viewed through the eyes of an uninstructed spectator, the causes of Byron's matrimonial catastrophe seemed comparatively obvious; Annabella Milbanke, a blue-stocking débutante and an heiress into the bargain, a high-minded, slightly pretentious, maybe rather frigid girl, had determined that she would marry a celebrated poet and reform a well-known rake. Not unexpectedly, her ambitious project had failed; marriage had merely shown Don Juan in his most aggressive colouring; and there was little more that need be said.

* These conflicts took their name from the sling (*fronde*) with which Parisian urchins used to combat the police.

Since 1816, however, a great deal of miscellaneous information has thrown fresh light upon the story. It was far more complex than its early critics supposed; and the state of mind in which Annabella deserted the poet was not so simple and straightforward as some biographers would have us think. Her experience of marriage, we now learn, had not been uniformly wretched, but had included passing joys. Although, both morally and emotionally she often condemned Byron, physically she clung to him, until, having escaped at last from his magnetic presence, she decided she must break the spell. This was an aspect of the problem that bewildered her husband. How could she, he demanded, have persisted in rejecting and abandoning him when – a fact she would surely not deny – they had remained on warmly conjugal terms throughout the gloomiest periods of their married life, and, indeed, until the day they parted? 'Were you then *never* happy with me?' he wrote. '. . . Have no marks of affection, of the warmest and most reciprocal attachment, passed between us? or did . . . hardly a day go down without some such on one side and generally on both?'

During hours of crisis Byron's attitude was seldom consistent; nor was he always strictly disingenuous; but here, it seems, he spoke the truth. Their marriage, catastrophic in some respects, had unquestionably succeeded in another. Annabella's '*passions*', he had informed his elderly confidante, her worldly-wise aunt Lady Melbourne, not very long before his wedding, were a great deal stronger than they had either of them supposed; and, being himself an accomplished amorist, who may occasionally have taken hints from a novel he much admired, Choderlos de Laclos's *Les Liaisons Dangereuses*, clearly he did not hesitate to rouse them. Once aroused, they followed her into later life. During her long years of aggrieved, self-righteous widowhood, she appears often to have struggled against her own passionate impulses, which she did her best to disarm with the help of faith and good works. Leaving Byron, we know, had caused her exquisite anguish. As she passed his bedroom door – he had not risen to bid her or the child goodbye: he was then in what she called a 'fractious' mood – and caught sight of the mat on which his big Newfoundland dog slept, she had felt inclined, she remembered, to throw herself down there and 'wait at all hazards'. But the temptation, she added, had lasted 'only a moment'; and she had then fled towards the waiting carriage.

Annabella Byron, for the remainder of her life, was a deeply restive and unhappy woman, whose treatment of her wayward daughter, her solemn son-in-law and her unlucky grandchildren, though her intentions were always high-minded, did them incalculable harm. Hers could never have been a felicitous, even an enduring marriage; but it seems possible that, had she attached a greater value to the pagan joys of her youth, she might have grown old more benevolently. Here, nevertheless, as in many other married relationships, there are still aspects of the Byrons' situation that we cannot wholly understand. Marriage, says the Anglican prayer-book, is an 'excellent mystery'; and, although the word 'mystery', had, of course, quite another significance for a seventeenth-century bishop, the biographer who has investigated the strange married lives of certain famous married couples must admit that few marriages, ancient or modern, do not, now and then, deserve the epithet.

Below, for example, is a letter from another rakish poet to an injured wife that, unless perhaps they have seen it before, may very well perplex its readers:

> "'Tis not an easy thing to be entirely happy, but to be kind is very easy and that is the greatest measure of happiness. I say not this to put you in mind of being kind to me – you have practised that so long that I have a joyful confidence you will never forget it – but to show that I myself have a sense of what the methods of my life seem so utterly to contradict.'*

It was written, in fact, by John Wilmot, Earl of Rochester, whose methods of life, at that stage of his existence, about 1678 or 1679, were particularly destructive. His marriage, before he was twenty years old, to Elizabeth Malet, a young woman whom Grammont calls 'the melancholy heiress' and Pepys 'the great beauty and fortune of the North', had had a strange, dramatic prelude. On May 28th, 1665, Pepys was able to provide the wife of his cousin and patron, Lord Sandwich, with an interesting piece of London news – the heiress, while she drove home, accompanied by her

---

* From *The Letters of John Wilmot Earl of Rochester*, edited with an introduction by Jeremy Treglown, 1980.

grandfather, from a supper party at Whitehall, 'was at Charing-cross seized on by both horse and footmen, and forcibly taken from him, and put into a coach with six horses and two women, and carried away'. They were immediately pursued; 'my Lord of Rochester . . . was taken at the bridge; but the lady is not yet heard of, and the King mighty angry and the Lord sent to the Tower'.

Charles quickly forgave a favourite courtier, but commanded that he should now join a naval expedition against the coast of Holland, and, although the plan itself proved a costly failure, and two of his friends were shot down beside him on the quarter-deck, he played his part with great distinction. Later that same year, he was appointed a Gentleman of the Bedchamber, a position supposed to carry the generous fee, though it was seldom regularly paid, of a thousand pounds per annum. Then, in January 1667, the heiress, just why none of their acquaintances could tell, suddenly decided that she might accept his hand. Perhaps the kidnapping was a romantic adventure she had thoroughly enjoyed; and no doubt he was a far more seductive young man than any of her previous suitors, 'my Lord Herbert . . . my Lord Hinchinbroke . . . my Lord John Butler', even Sir Francis Popham, who 'would kiss her breech to have her', she had once self-confidently declared.

Rochester's portraits, the canvas by an unknown artist that represents him, his sword at his belt, leaning negligently on his left elbow, and the fantastic picture that shows him crowning his monkey with a laurel wreath, depict a curiously handsome face, well-suited to the baroque curls of an exuberant Restoration wig. The nose is pointed and long; the eyes are heavily lidded; and the full, sensuous mouth has a slightly feminine look, which reminds us that, according to his poems* and his letters, his sexual inclinations were very often paederastic. Rochester's record as a 'rake-hell', the perpetrator of endless freaks and follies, which ranged from smashing the King's sundial in the Privy Garden, because, he alleged, it had an impertinently phallic shape, to fighting the watch and running naked through Woodstock Park, a royal demesne of which he had just been appointed Ranger, often startled and shocked his contemporaries, whose indignation was not easily aroused. For Pepys, a conscientious civil

* See, for example, 'The Disabled Debauchee', in *The Complete Poems of John Wilmot, Earl of Rochester*, edited by David M. Vieth, 1968.

Rochester, poet and rake-hell, proposes to crown his monkey with a laurel-wreath; portrait by J. Huysmans.

servant, Rochester typified everything he found discreditable about the lazy sovereign's raffish favourites; and, in February, 1669, he heard an unusually scandalous story: when the King had dined last night at the Dutch Ambassador's and after dinner they had drunk and 'were pretty merry', Rochester boxed Tom Killigrew's ears, 'which doth both much give much offence to the people here at Court, to see how cheap the King makes himself, and the more for that the King hath not only passed by the thing and pardoned it to Rochester already, but this very morning the King did publicly walk up and down, and Rochester I saw with him, as free as ever, to the King's everlasting shame to have so idle a rogue his companion'.

Here Pepys, it is true, seems for once to have been somewhat ill-informed. As a result of this escapade, Rochester, we know, was temporarily banished from the Court; and his behaviour, a fellow courtier admitted, was not altogether inexcusable, since Killigrew had abused him 'for keeping his wife in the country'; and his marriage – he had been wedded only two years – was presumably a topic on which he would have very much resented drunken dinner-table jokes. At the time, he still hoped to reconcile the claims of his London life with his domestic obligations, and possibly thought that he might yet succeed. But his failure soon became obvious. Rochester was a natural extremist, whose pursuit of new pleasures and violent sensations, complicated by his avid thirst for knowledge – always an omnivorous reader, he took a special interest in works of philosophy and theology – allowed him very little peace; and, at the age of thirty-three, he was already an exhausted man. Meantime, he told Bishop Burnet, the ghostly counsellor who attended his death-bed, 'for five years together he was continually Drunk: not all the while under the visible effect of it', but not cool enough to be perfectly 'Master of himself'. Once he had quitted the country, he felt his nature change; 'he was wont to say', wrote the ever-informative John Aubrey, 'that when he came to Brentford the devill ent'red with him and never left him till he came into the country again'.

Yet the devil that then possessed him, though it may have hastened his physical ruin, was also a creative daimon; and during his riotous course he produced a series of the finest lyrics written by an English poet in the later

seventeenth century. Some, it appears, were addressed to his wife at home; some to Elizabeth Barry,* his unruly mistress; some have an odd devotional colouring. Here fidelity was very often his theme, together with the unaccountable ambivalence of human feelings, and the difficulty of fixing one's emotions upon a single worthy object. If he cannot be constant in his own life, neither does he expect unwavering constancy from the woman he desires:

> 'Tis not that I am weary grown
> Of being yours, and yours alone:
> But with what face can I incline
> To damn you to be only mine?
> You, whom some kinder power did fashion,
> By merit, and by inclination,
> The joy at least of a whole nation.

Yet Rochester's dread of losing the emotional refuge he sought, and sometimes he hoped he might have found, seems to have endlessly tormented him:

> . . . When wearied with a world of woe,
> To thy safe bosom I retire,
> Where love and peace and truth does flow
> May I contented there expire.
>
> Lest once more wandering from that Heaven,
> I fall on some base heart unblest,
> Faithless to thee, false, unforgiven,
> And lose my everlasting rest.

Between Rochester and his wife and their young children, an only son and three daughters, the bond remained unbroken till his death. He was a warmly affectionate parent, who, in the many letters he wrote Lady

---

* One of the stars of the Restoration stage, Mrs Barry was seen at her best in the plays of Thomas Otway, who had desperately loved her, and whose masterpiece *Venice Preserv'd* was first produced in 1682.

Rochester, usually included tender messages to the nursery, and sometimes added 'great and glorious' gifts, among them a puppy from the royal
kennels, intended for his heir, Lord Wilmot, which, to amuse the boy, he
described as 'a dog of the last litter of lap-dogs so much reverenced at
Indostan', where they 'lie on cushions of cloth of gold at the feet of the
Great Mogul'. Yet more significant is an elaborate lyric dialogue,
composed by husband and wife, which shows that Lady Rochester herself,
besides being a sensitive and intelligent woman, was a gifted minor poet;
and in her contribution* she half-apologises for the mask of severity that,
since 'kindness' has again and again failed, she sometimes feels obliged to
wear —

> Though you still possess my heart,
> Scorn and rigor I must feign;
> There remains no other art
> Your love, fond fugitive, to gain.

— while the fugitive replies that it is for kindness he still yearns, and protests
that, come what may, he is inescapably her prisoner:

> Ah! Be kinder, then, for I
> Cannot change, and would not die.

The Rochesters' marriage, in short, was one of those unions it would be
wrong to call 'happy', yet from which happiness was never completely
absent. Like Byron, the poet must have recognised that his character was
fast changing, and that, at least until his physical strength gave way and, on
his death-bed, he took refuge in religious repentance, he had an anarchic,
yet creative spirit that refused to be expelled. Such ill-balanced marriages,
seen through a biographer's eyes, are often particularly absorbing; but
they become most memorable should their story exhibit the conflict of two
gifted, though very different personalities, whom their ignorance, both of
themselves and of one another, dooms to a protracted union where each

* The lines, of which some are quoted here, have been preserved in the authoress's own
script.

develops, not perhaps into a determined foe, yet certainly into an obstinate antagonist. That, for example, was the destiny of Thomas and Jane Carlyle. After considering the problems of a Restoration poet, to leap across the centuries and review the difficulties of a puritanical Victorian prophet may seem a somewhat hazardous adventure. But marriage, as an institution, has many aspects, good and bad alike, that recur in every age; and, as the Carlyles were both keen observers of the world, and each had a fine descriptive gift, their joint chronicle provides a more elaborately detailed picture of domestic happiness and misery than almost any similar record published during the last three hundred years.

Not only were they remarkably different characters; but they had entered adult life and approached wedlock by completely separate paths. For Carlyle it had been a hard way, so seldom enlivened by happiness that he remembered with a peculiar gratitude the few occasions when the clouds had lifted. This he had known in his early manhood, at an old farmhouse named Hoddam Hill, which had then afforded him a contemplative refuge from the world. The year he passed there, he afterwards wrote, lay in his memory 'like a not ignoble russet-coated Idyll – I lived very silent, diligent, had long solitary rides'. But, during those months, he found 'that I had conquered all my scepticisms, agonising doubtings, fearful wrestlings with the foul and vile and soul-murdering Mud-gods of my Epoch . . . and was emerging, free of spirit, into the eternal blue of ether . . . and, for a number of years, had, in spite of nerves and chagrins, a constant inward happiness that was quite royal and supreme . . .'

At the same period, however, he was already carrying on a lengthy, argumentative, yet affectionate correspondence with a well-educated and well-brought-up girl he hesitantly planned to marry. Jane Baillie Welsh had had an agreeable youth. An 'ex-spoilt' child, a blue-stocking and social belle, said to be equally proud 'of her Latin and her eye-lashes', she admired and respected the rough-edged peasant-scholar, yet remained, for the moment at least, perfectly conscious of the gulf that lay between them. Why she had at last crossed it she would explain, after many years of marriage, to a favourite cousin Jeannie Welsh. Her reasons, she admitted, had not been wholly idealistic. But, merely because he was 'the least

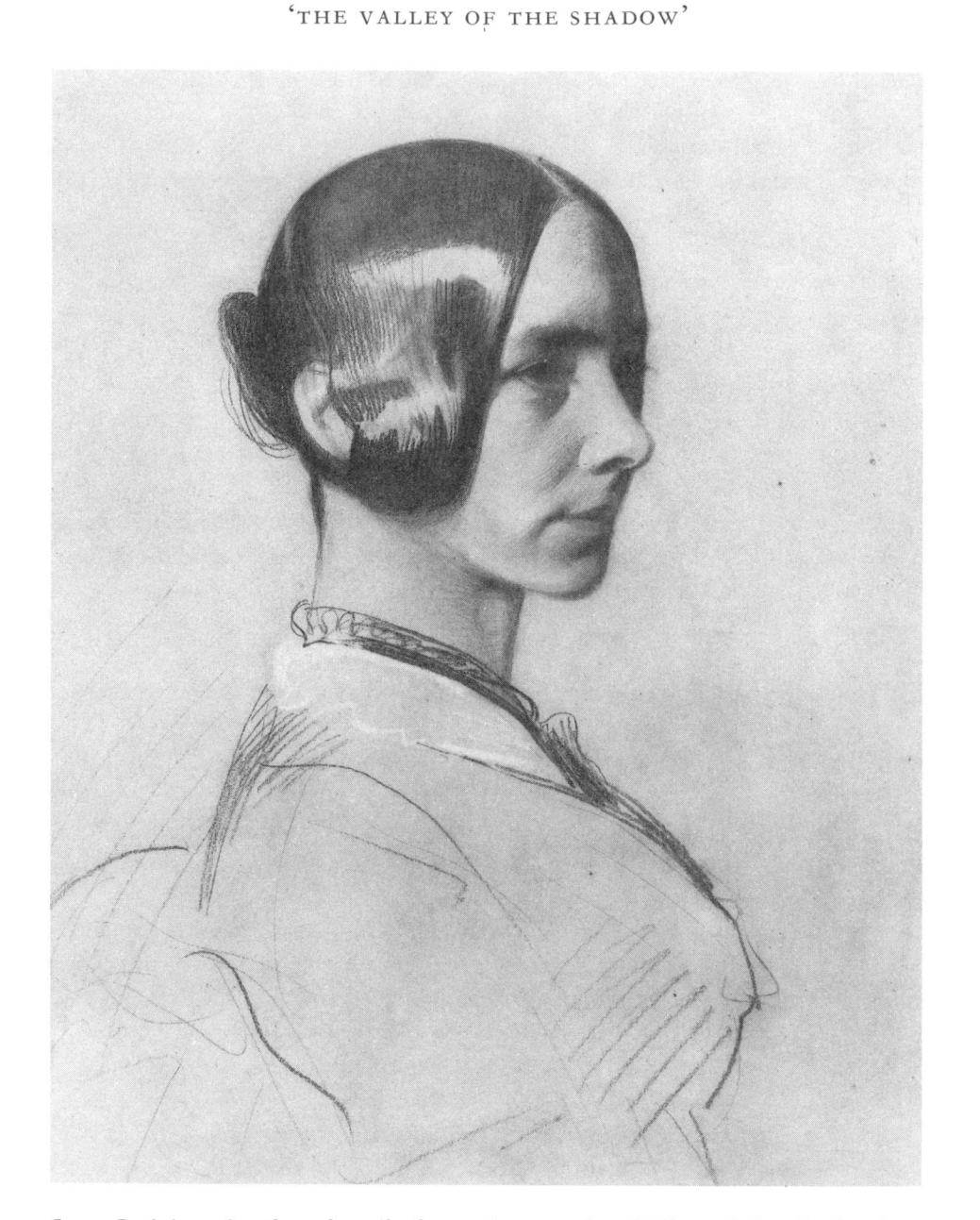

Jane Carlyle, who first described marriage as the 'Valley of the Shadow'.
Portrait by Samuel Laurence.

unlikable man in the place, I let him dance attendance on my young person, till I came to *need* him – all the same as my slippers to go to a ball, or my bonnet to go out to walk. When I finally agreed to marry him, I *cried* excessively and felt excessively shocked – but if I had then said *no* he would have left me.'

Feminine self-absorption, of which Jane Carlyle had her full share, has seldom been so candidly revealed; and she could not have known that Carlyle, too, had had secret doubts, which grew more and more oppressive as he approached his wedding day. Nor did the first night of marriage help to raise his troubled spirits. Next morning, 'sick with sleeplessness, quite nervous . . . splenetic and all the rest of it', he was sufficiently distraught to seek the professional advice of his brother Dr John; for he was still 'in a maze', he reported, 'scarce knowing the right from the left in the path I have to walk'. He begged, nevertheless, that John would reassure their anxious mother, telling her that 'I do believe I shall get *hefted* [adjusted] to my new situations, and then be one of the happiest men alive'.

Whether such an adjustment was ever successfully made is a question that we cannot answer. Since James Froude, his literary executor, first informed Carlyle's readers that their hero had suffered from lifelong impotence, it has been frequently proposed. But, although there is no doubt that Carlyle was a man to whom passionate love meant very little – he might have agreed with a modern poet, the late Philip Larkin, who once declared that he regarded 'sexual recreation as a socially remote thing, like baccarat or clog-dancing' – it is evident that, whatever his physical shortcomings may have been, he did not lack emotional strength, and that, in its later stages, their long, difficult alliance – earlier, they had passed through a devastating storm – would finally come to rest on a solid basis of affection and esteem. Jane was convinced she had married a great writer, whose interests she shared and whose sufferings she understood; while Carlyle listened appreciatively to her brilliant talk, and admired her as not only the most graceful, but the most practically accomplished woman – she alone could defend him against builders, painters, tax-collectors and noisy neighbours – who had ever come his way.

Where they constantly differed was in their attitude towards the outer world. Carlyle detested the society into which he had been born, and

abhorred and feared its loathsome 'Mud-gods'. Jane had a keenly social nature; she was fond of her fellow men and women, and all the more attached should they, besides engaging her affections, excite her gift of lively ridicule. A truly absurd personage, for example, the wild Italian artist Spiridione Gambardella, she found immediately sympathetic. Carlyle, on the other hand, though he is said to have once laughed aloud at Emerson delivering a lecture, did not smile easily; of an antagonist he seldom made fun; and to light-hearted derision he preferred stentorian reproof. If he esteemed certain contemporaries, it was because he thought he had detected in them high ambitions, coupled with an intellect and a strength of creative purpose, that he recognised as not unlike his own. Lastly, there was the eternal problem of happiness, to which Jane tentatively and wistfully aspired, and Carlyle, if it were regarded as a serious aim in life, always angrily dismissed. At the age of forty-three, when a philosophic German friend, Plattnauer, nicknamed 'Plato', who had for a while vanished, and then, out of the blue, written to inform Jane that he had now been completely restored and become the 'happiest of human beings', she congratulated him 'on having arrived at happiness by whatsoever inconceivable means', but added that she was apt to receive statements of this kind *'with a superstitious shudder – Happiness if there was such a thing at all seeming to me of the nature of those delicate spirits which vanish when one pronounces their name.'*

Yet it is hard to believe that the elusive spirit did not sometimes visit her at the pleasant Queen Anne house, No. 5 Great Cheyne Row (today No. 24 Cheyne Row), where she had long entertained, and was conscious of having delighted and amused, so many odd and celebrated guests. For Carlyle, a laborious cenobite, the house he inhabited was primarily a cave, in which, from the huge mass of relevant material, written and printed, that always accumulated on his desk, he struggled to weave a single strong thread of historic or prophetic meaning. For Jane, however, who cherished her private background, and did all she could to beautify it, her own house was the stage on which she looked and talked her best, and the setting of endless human dramas. There Mazzini and Godefroi Cavaignac, both distinguished exiles, and each apparently a little in love with her, found their favourite refuge at her feet; while Charles Dickens, also a

Thomas Carlyle produced most of his books, he said, 'in a state seldom enlivened by happiness', but often in a 'period of deep gloom and dubitation'. Crayon portrait by Laurence.

platonic devotee, listened to the strange stories she told them about 'The House of Mysteries' next door, and assured her that, if she decided to employ her literary talents, she would make a gifted novelist. No less interesting and picturesquely varied were the visitors that Carlyle himself attracted, among them Emerson, the homespun Bostonian sage, and Count d'Orsay, the prince of London dandies, who arrived wearing exquisitely skin-tight pantaloons, numerous gold chains, and generally glistening like a diamond beetle.

It was behind the scenes, before the first admirers had arrived or after the last had gone, that 'the Valley of the Shadow of Marriage' – a phrase that Jane employed in a letter to her cousin – when one personality had room to grind against the other, might seem almost unendurable. After her death, looking back with a widower's bitter remorse on the forty years that he and Jane had shared, Carlyle would describe them as a 'sore life-pilgrimage'; and, although a succession of different problems, including his lack of sexual and emotional sympathy, had helped to make their pilgrimage more grievous, the fact that he so seldom derived any real happiness from his labours was possibly the worst of all. Only the enthusiastic reviews that, in 1837, greeted *The French Revolution* had afforded him 'wild gleamings of a strange joy', followed twelve months later by 'a sense of peacable joy', which, he characteristically admitted, did not long remain with him. Otherwise, his major works, *Frederick the Great*, *The Letters and Speeches of Oliver Cromwell* and his controversial volume *Latter-Day Pamphlets*, the product, he said, of a 'period of deep gloom and dubitation', would appear to have brought him, while he laboured in his sound-proof room, little but daily anguish and despair.

Yet, not until 1842, when Carlyle was nearly fifty, and Jane forty-three, did a violent emotional tempest shake the foundations of their marriage; and this crisis, in various guises, with many lulls and fresh outbursts, dragged on nearly fifteen years. Its origins were unforeseeable. Jane had long believed, and had sometimes assured her friends, that to women *'as women'* Carlyle remained totally indifferent. Yet, in middle age, he developed a disturbing passion for a celebrated London hostess. Lady Harriet Baring

(later Lady Ashburton) was herself already thirty-seven; and when they first met, he noted that, although 'full of mirth and spirit', and 'one of the cleverest creatures' he had yet encountered, she was 'not very beautiful to look upon'; for she had an engaging, quickly intelligent face, but a substantial Junoesque figure and a short, square nose that even her admirers said somehow reminded them of Thackeray.

Carlyle's passion for his 'Sovereign Lady', his 'Queen', his 'Daughter of the Harmonies' and 'Daughter of the Sun', seems to have been exalted and imaginative rather than, in the ordinary sense, physical; and thus, confronted with a woman he adored, but to whom he had none of the sexual obligations he knew he could not properly fulfil in marriage, he felt free to revive some of the romantic daydreams he had harboured since his lonely youth. It was the romantic, even phantasmagoric character of his affection that most tormented and perplexed his wife. And then, to increase her woes, she could not refrain from secretly respecting and admiring her rival. An accomplished *femme du monde*, Lady Harriet was so versed in the ways of the world, and so subtle a diplomatist, that, because she enjoyed her 'dear old Prophet's' company and his fascinating table-talk, she refused to give his clever life-companion the smallest excuse for appearing neglected and aggrieved.

Nothing she did or said, however, could permanently ease Jane's heartache or Carlyle's dark nostalgic longings. He would gladly attend a fashionable ball that the Sovereign Lady held; but, once he had returned home, for all the 'divine benevolence' she had shown him there, he was immediately struck down by an overwhelming sense of deprivation:

'You gave us a glorious Ball . . . It is something to have seen such a one, and been seen by her – though only as if from precipice to precipice, with horrid chasms, and roaring cataracts, and black rivers of Acheron flowing between, forever! . . . I will call tomorrow, about four; can stay half an hour . . .'

The story of this strange episode in the Carlyles' relationship has already been sensibly and sympathetically related;* but here its pacific sequel most

* Best of all by Iris Origo in her account of 'A Victorian Friendship', *A Measure of Love*, 1957.

concerns us. Carlyle's feelings lost their dangerous strength; Jane slowly recovered her hold on life; and her confidence that she still kept Carlyle's love was, at length, successfully restored. Then, in 1857, Lady Ashburton died, having shown to the end her usual gaiety and courage; and meanwhile, at overcast Cheyne Row, a reconciliation had begun to dawn. Each of the contestants was prepared to admit some faults. Jane, for example, agreed that she was occasionally a poor companion: 'God knows how gladly I would be sweet-tempered and cheerful-hearted . . . if my temper were not soured and my heart saddened, beyond my own power to mend them'; and Carlyle patiently assured her that she had never lost his love, although she might fail to understand his problems: 'You know nothing about me just now. With all the clearness of vision you have, your lynx-eyes do not reach the inner vision of me, and know now what is in my heart . . . I wish you did; I wish you did.'

By April 1865, peace, so far as they were capable of experiencing it, had settled on the Carlyles' household. Jane had put behind her eighteen months of an exquisitely painful psychosomatic illness,* and Carlyle was offered the Lord Rectorship of Edinburgh University, one of the few public honours he was ready to accept. Both were gratified; but neither, of course, escaped anxiety; and Jane's apprehensions were particularly acute. Carlyle, she knew, was expected to address the assembled university; and, once he had set out, she suffered great alarm not from 'over anxiety', she wrote, 'about the success of the speech when spoken, but from a wild idea that it might never get spoken at all, that what with previous sleeplessness and wild hubbub . . . and the whole unsuitability of the thing, when he rose up to speak he might probably . . . *drop down dead*!' Her fears were groundless; Carlyle's speech, as a telegram from Edinburgh soon informed her, had been unquestionably 'A Perfect Triumph'. Discarding the notes he had made, but afterwards decided that he would not use, Carlyle spoke for an hour-and-a-half – on his youth at this same university, on his later life, his struggles and his doubts, and then advised the listening

---

* It had begun with a painful accident, when she was knocked down in the street; but its after-effects seem to have bewildered her doctors, one of whom declared that he could not contend against 'hysterical' mania.

students how to prosecute their own researches, to read thoroughly and carefully, think calmly and oppose the false gods of the present age. During his speech he made several references to Goethe. Carlyle, as a rule, mistrusted poets; their behaviour was usually loose; their principles were vague and self-destructive. But Goethe was a grand exception, a master-poet who was also a prophet and a teacher, and whose view of the universe was supremely solemn. 'Awe', he had told the world, 'was the highest thing in man'; and if, a man experienced that, he should be content; he could be aware of nothing higher.

Carlyle shared that sense of awe. What had been denied him, however, was Goethe's delight in the natural world and eager wide-ranging curiosity about every manifestation of life that met his eye – a school of dolphins, their colours changing from gold to green, and then from green to gold, as they leapt across the waves; or a Sicilian garden, where he revived his 'old fancy' concerning the origin of species, and hoped perhaps to distinguish the basic forms, the *Urphänomene*, of all the flowers and plants he loved. Carlyle had neither Goethe's capacity for keen sensuous enjoyment nor the breadth of his poetic vision; but both believed that suffering was an important part of human experience, which quickened and enriched the soul; and at Edinburgh in 1886 he quoted not only Goethe's message of hope and comfort; but some lines he had himself translated:

> Who never ate his bread in sorrow,
> Who never spent the midnight hours
> Weeping and waiting for the morrow,
> He knows you not, ye Heavenly Powers

Meanwhile, Jane, having heard of Carlyle's magnificent reception, hastened to express her pride and love; but this letter, headed simply 'Dearest', and one of the most affectionate and least querulous she had written him for many years, also proved to be her valediction; for on April 23rd, John Ruskin, who was about to leave England and had called at Cheyne Row to bid her goodbye, was met by a weeping maid-servant on the threshold with the news that Mrs Carlyle had died a few hours earlier, suddenly and peacefully in her own carriage as she drove round Hyde Park.

I0

'The Golden World'

WITH the pursuit of happiness goes the quest for the Heavenly City or the Terrestrial Paradise; and, when Samuel Johnson announced that complete felicity was discoverable only in our recollections or in our expectations, he might have added that the place where a man at present finds himself is seldom altogether to his liking. Visions of 'Somewhere Else' – 'N'importe où hors du monde': 'Anywhere out of the World'* – have haunted poets since imaginative literature began; and, although a few have written contentedly and gratefully of their own immediate surroundings – Horace often praises his little Sabine farm – others, Baudelaire and Leopardi, for example, have regarded the present-day world as, if not a gaol, at least a penal colony, in which they were condemned to serve. Worldly success and the free enjoyment of power do not necessarily appease a restive spirit. Alexander the Great, we are told, never ceased hankering for new frontiers to cross and fresh kingdoms to invade; and among dynasts Shah Jehan alone, most sympathetic of the Mughal Emperors, seems to have escaped a secret malaise. 'Should there indeed be a paradise one earth,' he exclaimed, looking out over Delhi from his magnificent Red Fort, 'it is this. Oh, it is this! It is surely this!'

As the poetic account of an expedition to a far-off country where happiness and harmony reign, Homer's description of Odysseus's visit to the Land of the Phaeacians is probably the earliest and the best. On his way home after

* Baudelaire gives his prose poem both a French and an English title.

[137]

capturing and sacking Troy, the hero had suffered grim vicissitudes, exposed to the martial ferocity of the Cicones and the Laestrigonians and the primitive brutality of the cannibalistic giant Polyphemus; and then, once he had reached Ogygia, the island home of the enchantress Calypso, held in amorous captivity for several long unhappy years, until Hermes, messenger of the Olympian Gods, carrying his golden wand of office, had demanded she should set him free.

On the stout raft that Odysseus therefore builds himself, and that Calypso generously provisions with fresh water, wine and corn, he yet again becomes a wanderer; but he has forgotten that he has a divine enemy, the powerful sea-god Poseidon; a huge wave soon destroys his raft; and, naked, exhausted, scurfed with sea-salt, he is cast ashore upon an unknown beach. There a stroke of brilliant good fortune awaits him; he meets the virginal princess Nausicaa, busy at the time with the pile of household laundry she and her maids have brought down in a mule-cart to the river-bank. Nausicaa is one of literature's most delightful and endearing heroines. Brave and free-spoken, she has also the gift of beauty, which Odysseus, exhausted though he is, quickly recognises and eloquently acclaims. She reminds him, he says, of a young tree he had seen in other days growing at Delos beside the altar of Apollo; and he marvels at her, and fears to approach her and touch her knees as a proper suppliant should have done. But Nausicaa calmly reassures him, summons her frightened maids, commands them to bring him food and wine, and provide a tunic and a cloak from the garments they have just laid out to dry. She is the daughter, she explains, of Alcinous, sovereign of the Phaeacians, a people the Olympian Gods especially love, who dwell on the utmost verges of the earth, far beyond contact with ordinary men.

Half a century ago, to rehearse the story of Odysseus's meeting with Nausicaa might very well have seemed impertinent; but now that neither Homer's text nor Pope's vigorous translation (praised by Johnson as 'the noblest version of poetry that the world has ever seen'*) is still an essential part of any good library, this enchanting fairy-tale may perhaps be a little less familiar. Homer does not depict Nausicaa's beauty in detail, giving us

* The famous scholar Dr Bentley, on the other hand, once remarked to the translator: 'It's a very pretty poem, Mr Pope, but you mustn't call it Homer.'

her carriage, the line of her youthful cheeks and chin, the colour of her eyes and hair. These the reader himself must recreate; and, although at other periods he would probably have visualised her as a smooth Praxitelean nymph or, later, as a Graeco-Roman demi-goddess, today she recalls a member of the bewitching family of *Korai*, the band of graceful girls, statues of ministrants carrying votive offerings to Athene's shrine,* whom we admire today on the Acropolis. They are slender and straight-limbed; their long locks are invariably braided and curled; and all have the same subtly enigmatic expression, the corners of their mouths slightly turned up, that archaeologists have labelled 'the Archaic smile'.

To Nausicaa's home, the palace of her father Alcinous, its remoteness lends a particular distinction; the Phaeacians admit they are emigrants; harried in their native country by Polyphemus' monstrous kinsmen, they have withdrawn to their present remote land where they are safe against their foes. The Gods moreover have favoured them, and they have developed extraordinary skills; 'their ships are as swift as the flight of a bird or as a thought', so that their seamen have ceased to depend on pilots or rudders; their craft themselves understand the sailor's purpose. Given these blessings, the Phaeacians are a quiet, contented race and lead modestly luxurious lives; 'for we', their ruler assures Odysseus, whom, after some diplomatic questioning, he has accepted as an honoured guest, 'are not skilled boxers or wrestlers, but fast runners and good seamen, and dear to us always are feasting and music, the dance and frequent changes of clothing, and the warm bath and love and sleep.'

I remember how much in my youth, 'doing Greek' at an English public school at which athleticism was highly valued, this evocation of the Phaeacian way of life appealed to me. Homer must certainly have admired it. Whether he was a single poet, or the skilled editor and co-ordinator of a host of ancient legends, he is now believed to have worked during the seventh or eighth century B.C., and to be looking back at a state of society, based perhaps on recollections of the glorious Mycenaean Age, that had no longer any real existence.† Alcinous' palace with its brazen threshold and

---

* They were probably carved about six centuries before Christ, and desecrated during the Persian invasion.
† See M.I. Finley: *The World of Odysseus,* 1956.

walls, surmounted by a bright blue frieze, its golden statues of youths and hounds, and the orchards and gardens that encompass it, must undoubtedly have borne some resemblance to the ruins of a Mycenaean palace recently excavated at Pylos (the modern Navarino) where Telemachus, in quest of news about Odysseus, discovers the venerable Nestor and his subjects sacrificing black bulls on the sea-shore to the Earth-Shaker Poseidon; for there we find both a noble bathroom and the kind of circular open hearth Alcinous' consort Areté sits beside with her maidservants, spinning skeins of purple wool. Thus, Phaeacia is a romantic Utopia or Never-Never Land, and represents life not as it was when Homer immortalised its ancient splendour, but as a beautifully organised society in which human happiness - Alcinous feels proud of his people's welfare – is among a sovereign's chief concerns.

The whole episode has a lyrical and nostalgic colouring: and, when I read Homer's description of Nausicaa, I have sometimes thought of a far later and less classic heroine. *A Winter's Tale* is not Shakespeare's most expertly balanced comedy; it includes too many ill-assorted elements, for example, a slightly preposterous transformation scene, the unveiling of Hermione, no doubt devised to please the new-fangled Jacobean taste. The play, first seen in 1611 and acted before King James the same year, is a product of Shakespeare's last phase, which also gave us *The Tempest*; and, like that fascinating work, it suggests that the poet's state of mind when he wrote it, was not altogether tranquil; it contains such alarming reflections of jealousy, cruelty and tyranny; and it is from them that the dramatist at last escapes when Prince Florizel approaches the Shepherd's cottage, now the home of Perdita, the lost princess.

This was not the only romantic refuge from the hardships of real life that the poet had presented. In 1599 or 1600 he had written *As You Like It*, where his background is the Forest of Arden, named after his mother's dignified land-owning family, whither the old Duke and his cheerful companions have retired to follow Robin Hood's example, and 'fleet the time carelessly, as they did in the golden world'. That world is an anticipation of the Earthly Paradise; and there a seeker after happiness, temporarily at least, is well protected against the harsher and uglier aspects of ordinary life. Between 1599 and 1611, Shakespeare himself had lived

A Greek girl, wearing the typical 'Archaic smile'; one of the statues of Athene's ministrants, now in the Acropolis Museum.

[141]

through a succession of painful crises, and produced the tremendous tragedies of what critics call his 'Dark Period'. In 1601, Essex and Shakespeare's patron and friend Southampton had staged their abortive revolt, which came to a catastrophic end: and, while Essex had paid with his life on the scaffold, Southampton had suffered close confinement in the Tower, which would last until the old Queen's death. Even worse was the sequel; eager loyalists, anxious both to protest their own devotion and share in the spoils of the favourite's disgrace, had loudly begged for their reward. Human cupidity and falsehood had seldom been so miserably displayed.

In *A Winter's Tale* Shakespeare seems for a moment to cut free from the real world; and his story and treatment of it alike have a deliberately fictitious turn. Bohemia is given a sea-coast; an inexplicable bear suddenly emerges, and chases Antigonus back into the wings. Few details, once we have reached Act IV – Act I contains a realistic and extraordinarily moving picture of Leontes' affection for his son and jealous attachment to his wife – are not playfully fantastic. 'This is fairy gold, boy,' says the Shepherd, 'and 'twill prove so', fairy gold being a stuff that pleases the eye, and very soon afterwards dissolves. But, although the Shepherd's cottage is situated in the land of legends, one of the occupants has an unconquerably vital spirit. Perdita is no mere poetic wraith; and, almost as soon as she emerges, we hear her voice and, like Odysseus confronting Nausicaa, quickly recognise her wit and beauty. Odysseus compared the Phaeacian princess to a young tree; and Perdita in movement, Florizel exclaims, has the grace of an ocean wave:

> '. . . when you do dance, I wish you
> A wave o' the sea that you might do
> Nothing but that; and move still, still so,
> And own no other function . . .'

She has all her period's most engaging traits – its passion for flowers, its appreciation of fine language and its unblushing lack of prudery. She does not conceal the romantic attraction that draws her irresistibly towards Florizel; and, when she delivers the incomparable speech in which she enumerates the flowers, from spring daffodils to 'the flower-de-luce', that she wishes she could strew about him, and Florizel protests 'What, like a corse?', she replies with delightful boldness:

'No, like a bank for love to lie and play on;
Not like a corse . . .
But quick and in mine arms. Come, take your flowers.'

All the inhabitants of Shakespeare's Bohemia are bohemians in the modern meaning of the word – rebels who stubbornly reject convention and obey their own rebellious instincts. Seen through the eyes of a Jacobean magistrate, Autolycus, the thievish pedlar, would have appeared an incorrigible 'rogue and vagabond'; not only does he sell his wares – 'ribands of all the colours i' the rainbow . . . inkles, caddisses,* cambrics, lawns' and 'sings 'em over as they were gods or goddesses' – during his rambles through the country; but he has also found a profitable sideline in pilfering the clean sheets that foolish housewives hang out upon the wayside hedges. Though his is a precarious and perilous existence, he keeps anxiety at bay: 'beating and hanging are terrors to me', he admits; yet for them, as 'for the life to come, I sleep out the thought of it'; and meanwhile he is perfectly content with the pleasures of the present hour:

> The lark that tirra-lirra chants,
> With heigh! with heigh! the thrush and the jay,
> Are summer songs for me and my aunts,
> While we lie tumbling in the hay.

– his 'aunts' being the rustic loves he has picked up on the road.

For Shakespeare and his contemporaries travel-books that reported the wonders of the New World were a constant source of inspiration. *The Tempest*, written about the same time as *A Winter's Tale*, derives both wise old Gonzalo's account of an Ideal Commonwealth and much of its romantic imagery from *A discovery of the Barmudas, otherwise called The Ile of Divels*; and writing both plays, he was also indebted to John Florio's translation of Montaigne's *Essays* that had been published in 1580. Here a chapter entitled 'Of Cannibals' is devoted to a primitive race, inhabitants of a remote Brazilian forest, who are 'wild just as we call wild the fruits that

---

* 'Inkles' are a kind of tape, 'caddisses' worsted ribbons.

Nature has produced herself', and barbarians only in so far as 'they have been fashioned very little by the human mind'. There follows a definition of happiness that recurs in varying forms throughout the *Essays*: 'To know how to enjoy our being rightfully, and to accept the terms of our own existence gladly, is the height of human wisdom.' Those are the gifts he imagined the Cannibals possessed; and the fact that his greatest friend, Etienne de la Boétie, had once thought of abandoning corrupt and over-civilised Europe for the natural pleasures of the New World he did not find at all surprising.

Although Montaigne himself was content to remain at home, jogging meditatively around his pleasant estate – it was in the saddle, he believed, that he thought most sensibly and clearly – or reading and writing in his turret room, where he had had painted on the beams the Delphic phrase 'Gnōthi Seauton', '*Know Thyself*', and some forty-nine other admonitory maxims, he shared the restive spirit of his age and its insatiable thirst for knowledge. Like an English poet, he identified this craving with all that is noblest in the human character:

> Nature, that fram'd us of four elements . . .
> Doth teach us all to have aspiring minds:
> Our souls, whose faculties can comprehend
> The wondrous architecture of the world,
> And measure every wand'ring planet's course,
> Still climbing after knowledge infinite,
> And always moving as the restless spheres,
> Will us to wear ourselves, and never rest . . .*

Christopher Marlowe, the Elizabethan *poète maudit*, who put these resounding, though oddly anachronistic lines into the mouth of Timour-Leng, the fourteenth-century Tartar war lord, was such an aspiring mind – so boldly and rashly speculative indeed that, just before his tragic death, he had aroused the suspicions of the Privy Council; while Sir Walter Ralegh, at whose so-called 'School at Night' he is said to have propounded his

---

* *Tamburlaine the Great*, Part I, Act II.

atheistic doctrines, was a no less adventurous climber after knowledge. Ralegh's aspirations as he summed them up in one of his own poems –

'To seek new worlds, for gold, for praise, for glory,
To try desire, to try love severed far'

– both determined his career at the Elizabethan Court, where he became a richly rewarded royal favourite, and presently carried him across the ocean to combine his search for the Golden City, the legendary El Dorado, with more romantic but almost equally elusive aims.

In 1595, he had an early glimpse of the unexplored Americas, and sighted not the Golden City, but, as he surveyed the banks of the Orinoco, an Arcadian landscape stranger and more romantic than any that had yet confronted him:

'I never saw a more beautiful country, nor more lively prospects, hills so raised here and there over the valleys, the river winding into divers branches, the plains adjoining without bush or stubble, all fair green grass, the ground of hard sand easy to march on either for horse or foot, the deer crossing in every path, the birds towards the evening singing on every tree with a thousand several tunes, cranes and herons of white, crimson and carnation perching on the river's side, the air fresh with a gentle, easterly wind, and every stone that we stooped to take up promised either silver or gold by his complexion.'*

It is characteristic of Elizabethan travellers that, besides enjoying the beauty of this Arcadian prospect, Ralegh and his companions should also have scrutinised the pebbles they saw at their feet for any trace of gold or silver; the English like the Spanish *conquistadores*, who, in their own search, soon ravished and destroyed the splendid civilisation of the great Mexican cities they had originally so much admired, were always ardently acquisitive; and on his last expedition to the New World Ralegh was still seeking the fabulous South American mine that, if discovered and exploited, would restore his credit with the King. His adventure failed; in

* *The Discoverie of Guiana.*

1618, an old charge of treason was revived, and he was thereupon condemned to death.

Once the legend of El Dorado had been finally abandoned, however, it was followed by a succession of other dreams; the New World was not the only region that now seemed to offer happiness. Even the Chinese Empire was regarded, temporarily at least, as an ancestral home of wisdom. English architects adopted Eastern modes, until, a critic complained, modern cowsheds and dairies had begun to develop strangely curvaceous roofs; while gardeners adapted the Chinese principle of design,* and skilled exponents of *chinoiserie* covered European walls and ceilings with imaginative representations of Far-Eastern landscapes, where bearded sages sat placidly smoking their pipes under elegant pavilions, amid their favourite disciples.

Thus, although the supposed location of the Earthly Paradise has varied considerably from age to age, when the United States had declared their independence it was the New World that, for the young Romantics, seemed again to offer special promise. Thither Chateaubriand's doomed hero, René, was to escape from the sins and sorrows of the old; and in 1794, the year Saint-Just described happiness as a 'new idea' that all revolutionary patriots were entitled to enjoy, the twenty-year-old Coleridge met Southey at Cambridge, and the two enthusiasts discussed the foundation of a self-governing Pantisocratic society, where every citizen would be free and equal. But such a society required a different political background; and, later that same summer, Coleridge, who then used to spend his nights in a London ale-house entitled the 'Salutation and Cat', drinking 'Porter and *Punch* round a good fire', happened to meet 'a most intelligent young man who has spent the last five years of his life in America – and is lately come from thence as an Agent to sell Land'.

He offered easy terms; two thousand pounds would probably be enough to establish the settlement that they intended:

'. . . For six hundred Dollars a thousand Acres may be cleared, and houses built upon them. He recommends the Susquehannah from its

* Known as 'Sharawadgi', it was first introduced by Sir William Temple in his essay *Upon the Gardens of Epicurus* (1685) and denoted the use of elegant irregularity.

[146]

excessive Beauty and its security from hostile Indians . . . Literary characters make money there . . . He never saw a Bison in his life, but has heard of them . . . The Mosquitoes are not so bad as our gnats – and after you have been there a little while, they don't trouble you much.'

Yet the enthusiasts would never set sail; by 1795 Coleridge decided, rightly no doubt, that their Pantisocratic Plan had done more credit to their hearts than to their heads. His affectionate association with Southey, however, had one disastrous result. Under its influence, he began to think of marriage, perhaps in the romantic Susquehannah country, and, having broken off an earlier engagement, he proposed to Sarah Fricker, sister of Southey's future wife – a young woman, he said, he had previously courted 'from principle, not feeling' – and met a reward that far exceeded 'the greatness of the effort: I love and am beloved, and I am happy.' Coleridge was by nature a moral theorist, and this discovery seemed to establish a point he had already once made: 'he cannot long be wretched who dares be actively virtuous.' But here he was very soon proved wrong. The Coleridges' marriage, though he begat children, and remained an intermittently domestic husband until 1806, brought them very little joy.

The impulse to leave home and found a new, more liberated and happier society that Coleridge and Southey failed to realise, has been shared by many English writers. In our own days, D.H. Lawrence spent much of his adult life on the same exhausting quest; and almost all his later novels describe the adventures of a different journey – to Tuscany, the Abruzzi, Mexico, New Mexico, Australia; and, whenever he could temporarily settle down, he hoped his best-loved associates might join him and build a spiritual haven, where the old conventional values would be discarded and the 'blood relationship' of man with man restored. Of these books, *The Plumed Serpent*, published thirteen years after his autobiographical masterpiece *Sons and Lovers*, is the strangest and the least appealing; for there, under the leadership of a typical Laurentian hero, Don Cipriano, a perfectly masculine man, 'a little fighting male', he depicts the dethronement of the Christian faith and the restoration of the ancient Aztec gods, Quetzalcoatal and the ferocious war-god Huitzilpochtli, whom Don Cipriano's followers acclaim with a typical Hitlerian salute. But Lawrence

[147]

the raucous prophet – T.S. Eliot called him a 'tin-chapel' orator – had a many-sided talent, and his love and understanding of the natural world far exceeded his comprehension of mankind. His personages, because they reflect his dogmas, prejudices and deep-rooted private obsessions, are often ill-drawn, even here and there grotesque; it is only when his theme is a landscape, a bird or a beast, and the strong effect they produce on his own imagination, that his genius seems to shine through.

The Spirit of Place, the splendid anthology of Lawrence's descriptive prose-writings made by Richard Aldington in 1944, is an endlessly illuminating work, and shows the pleasure that, like Coleridge, he derived from observation practised as a branch of literary art. It also suggests that, for him as for Rousseau in *Les Rêveries du Promeneur Solitaire*, the mere sense of being alive, which he had developed to so fine a point, and of having an integral link with the whole universe, might itself be happiness enough. Comparatively few modern English writers have had Lawrence's especial gift; but, during the Romantic Age,* both the Wordsworths – Dorothy in her prose jottings no less apparently than William in his verse – displayed the same aptitude for evoking the spirit, the other-worldliness or mythopoeic aspect, of a scene that they describe.

Here, for example, is Dorothy's description of the evening sky as she had watched it change from the threshold of Dove cottage:

> The vale looked as if it were filled with white light when the moon had climbed up to the middle of the sky; but long before we could see her face, while all the eastern hills were in black shade, those on the opposite side were almost as bright as snow. Mrs. Luff's large white dog lay in the moonshine upon the round knoll under the old yew-tree, a beautiful and romantic image – the dark tree with its dark shadow, and the elegant creature as fair as a spirit.

While she watched, the Terrestrial Paradise must have seemed momentarily very close indeed; and, although Nausicaa, Perdita and the Shepherd's

---

* The idea of Man's correspondence with Nature also fascinated the French Romantics. Thus Gérard de Nerval in *Aurélia*, his account of his own madness, relates how from every natural detail he observed '*Je voyait ressortir des harmonies jusqu'alors inconnues. "Comment" me disais-je "ai-je pu exister si longtemps hors de la nature et sans m'identifier à elle? Tout vit, tout agit, tout se correspond . . ."* '

Cottage, the Forest of Arden, where the old Duke and his companions fleeted the time away as men 'did in the golden world', even perhaps Ralegh's poetic vision of a great American river, are now fugitive 'fairy gold', almost every human being, once or twice in a lifetime, must have had a glimpse of an ideal universe, made for peace and happiness alone. Such recollections die hard; and I remember myself standing on a grassy Dorset cliff and looking down across a ten-mile stretch of brackish water named the Fleet, that here divides the coastline from a famous pebble ridge.* Not far off an ancient monastic swannery is still kept up by an enlightened landlord; and, as the sun was sinking, along the tranquil surface of the Fleet, which reflected a calm roseate sky, I saw a galaxy of swans drift past.

* One of the peculiarities of the Chesil Beach, said to be the most extensive in Great Britain, is that its pebbles, which vary in size from that of a pea to the dimensions of a small plate, are graded by the action of the tides; and we are told that, if a blind man who knew the Beach well were set down at any point, he could say exactly where he stood.

II

Paradise at a Stroke

I N the early nineteenth century, London maid-servants, who had just
begun their day's work, were very often seen hurrying towards a
nearby druggist's shop, where, for a shilling or less, they purchased a
large flagon of the clear purplish fluid named 'laudanum', a tincture of
opium with an admixture of alcohol, which at the time was as important a
part of the household pharmacopoeia as some harmless sedative today. It
had a dozen different uses; and Jane Austen records that, on a long
and tiring journey, her mother was advised by a local physician to take
'twelve drops . . . before she went to bed'. But, even at that period, its
excessive use was considered slightly dangerous; and Lady Byron, besides
deploring the poet's addiction to brandy, was also suspicious of the 'black
drops' she found in his dressing-room and among his travelling
equipment. Her alarm had little real foundation. Byron was excessive in
nearly everything he did. Laudanum, however, seems to have had no
decisive effect either on his work or on his personal character.

Others were less fortunate; and meanwhile for two of his gifted
contemporaries, Coleridge and Thomas De Quincey, the pleasures and
pains of opium-taking had developed a terrible significance. Each was a
fugitive, in flight not only from the trials of the present day but from a host
of oppressive recollections. Since his early youth, Coleridge remembered,
he had been 'most, MOST cruelly treated' by his unkind nurse and a sadistic
elder brother who acquired a taste for beating him; and at Cambridge he
first 'fled to Debauchery', next left his college and, having adopted a
grotesque pseudonym, enlisted in a British cavalry regiment, where,

unable to manage his charger or keep his equipment clean, he had proved absurdly unsuccessful.

De Quincey, too, had fled from the immediate problems of his life, and, deserting his respectable family, become a homeless wanderer around London; and both, at an early age, were introduced to opium, Coleridge before 1791, De Quincey in 1804 by a 'beatific' London druggist, the 'unconscious minister of celestial pleasures' and, at the same time, of unending miseries. But, like Coleridge, what he had originally sought was not happiness so much as relief from pain, in De Quincey's case 'excruciating rheumatic pains' that he had himself induced, having with a characteristic lack of good sense plunged his head into a basin of cold water and gone to bed without troubling to dry his hair.

The Confessions of an English Opium-Eater, published in 1821, is one of the most maddeningly diffuse and prolix books ever produced by a writer who, at his best, was a master of the language. De Quincey strays from theme to theme; his footnotes threaten to submerge the text; but then some wonderfully illuminating paragraph emerges, such as the poignant account – in my edition we must await it until page 177 – of how his addiction had long ago begun:

> 'It was a Sunday afternoon, wet and cheerless; and a duller spectacle this earth has not to show than a rainy Sunday in London. My way homeward lay through Oxford street; and I saw a druggist's. The druggist . . . looked dull and stupid . . . and when I asked for tincture of opium, he gave it to me . . . and furthermore, out of my shilling returned to me what seemed . . . real copper halfpence taken out of a real wooden drawer . . .'

As soon as he had regained his lodgings, he took the quantity prescribed. 'O heavens! What a revulsion! What a resurrection, from its lowest depths of the inner spirit!' Not only had his pain vanished; but 'this negative effect was swallowed up in the immensity of those positive effects which had opened up before me . . . Here was the secret of happiness, about which philosophers had disputed for so many ages . . . happiness might now be bought for a penny and carried in the waistcoat pocket . . .'

Although the druggist's shop probably existed – and some students claim they have discovered exactly where it must have stood – the whole story of De Quincey's introduction to opium has a somewhat dreamlike quality. In his world, as in Coleridge's, dreams, 'tumultuous dreams', played an exceedingly important part; and neither could easily decide where visions ended and 'real life' began. Very often they were aware of a closely interwoven pattern. In his sleep De Quincey was haunted by visions of his dear Ann, the 'noble-minded' young prostitute, who had kept him company and protected him in his London wanderings – again the background of the scene is Oxford Street – but, during his brief absence, had for ever disappeared. Coleridge was equally dream-obsessed, and liked to believe that the signs he thought he had received while he slept might sometimes prove to be celestial tokens. 'If a man could pass through Paradise in a dream', he noted on April 19th, 1817, 'and have a flower presented to him as a pledge that his soul had really been there, and if he found that flower in his hand when he awoke – Aye! and what then?'

While drug-addiction heightened the imagery of their dreams, which became beatific on the one hand and strangely terrifying and hideous upon the other, it encouraged and constantly frustrated the writers' search for individual happiness; and both had come close enough to their goal, and had viewed their objective with sufficient clarity to have a lasting sense of failure. It was as historic failures, sad survivors of a memorable past, that Carlyle described them in their later lives – Wordsworth's fallen hero, during his last retirement grown stout, flaccid, helplessly irresolute; and De Quincey seen as a talkative ageing man by the sharp-eyed, sharp-tongued pair at Cheyne Row:

'A pretty little creature, full of wire-drawn ingenuities; bankrupt enthusiasms, bankrupt pride; with the finest silver-toned low voice, and most elaborate gently winding courtesies . . . A bright, ready and melodious talker: but in the end an inconclusive and long-winded. One of the smallest man-figures I ever saw . . . When he sat, you would have taken him, in candlelight, for the beautifullest little Child . . . had there not been something too, which said "*Eccovi*, this Child has been in Hell".'

The Hell where Coleridge and De Quincey suffered was a very real inferno that they were condemned to enter almost every night of their latter-day existence. 'Sleep', Coleridge told his friend Tom Wedgwood, 'is my tormenting Angel . . . Dreams with me are no Shadows, but the very substances and foot-thick Calamities of my Life . . .'. As for De Quincey, he saw a close connection between his dreams with their strange scenery – 'the great lights and shadows' – and painful memories of his vagrant youth. But neither pretended that opium alone was the villain of his private drama. Opium, a modern literary historian writes in her excellent survey of *Opium and the Romantic Imagination,** was 'a symptom, not the cause' of Coleridge's downfall; and this seems equally true of the English Opium-Eater. Like other drugs, for example mescalin whose praises Aldous Huxley sang,† it does no more than accentuate the tendencies, and sometimes perhaps sharpen the vision, of an individual writer. It did not lead Coleridge directly to Xanadu, though if laudanum was the so-called 'anodyne' that, he explained, had plunged him into a profound sleep during which, 'without any sensation or consciousness of effort', he believed he had written the two to three hundred lines he was afterwards unable to transcribe in full, no doubt it started him along the road.

For the benefits he now and then received the penalty Coleridge paid was sometimes hideous. Yet opium, as the example of another writer shows, need not always be disruptive. During the same half-century, the poet George Crabbe, much admired by Wordsworth, Byron and Tennyson, who became an addict in his middle life, despite the nightmares it regularly provoked – he was vexed by a gang of ghostly ruffians he referred to as 'the Leather Lads', no doubt contemporary 'Hell's Angels' – long combined the habit with a highly successful poetic career and a calm domestic life. The only opium-taker I have myself observed at first-hand, an elderly South American diplomatist, seemed singularly well-preserved. Don Antonio shared De Quincey's reverence for the drug, and was delighted to learn that the famous English centenarian 'Old Parr' had habitually smoked or eaten it. He called it his *'bouillon de légumes'* and would leave a

* Alethea Hayter, 1968.
† *The Doors of Perception*, 1954.

[153]

party – he was a great party-goer – the moment he began to feel he needed it, but return, contented and sedate, within three quarters of an hour. I remember, when we were staying at the same house, having to walk through his room, where a scent-burner was smoking beside his bed, but I immediately detected the strong, unmistakable odour I had once enjoyed in Peking, a pungent vegetable fragrance, no more sinister or exotic than the smell of a hayfield on an English summer day.

I do not know if Don Antonio had read De Quincey; but Baudelaire's famous essay, *Les Paradis Artificiels*, which *The English Opium-Eater* had inspired, he must certainly have known. It recounts the poet's experiences at a period while, still a rebellious dandy, he occupied an apartment in the antique Hôtel Lauzun on the Ile Saint Louis; and he and his friends, including Théophile Gautier, held nightlong parties there for the sole purpose of experimenting with the hallucinatory effect of drugs, sometimes opium, but apparently more often *cannabis indica* or hashish. The two drugs, they soon learned, had completely different powers – hashish evoked large and grandiose scenes; opium induced a deep, delightful calm.* But Baudelaire and his fellow addicts, '*le Club des Haschisins*', had all very much the same objective; they planned to 'conquer Paradise at a stroke', and break into new realms of the imagination, by means of a mysterious chemical agent that would help them see the world anew. Compared with the extraordinary results they achieved, how simple, Baudelaire pointed out, was the apparatus that the Haschisins required! Itself it was nothing more than 'a green sweetmeat'. Yet there lay the secret of happiness, in something only 'large enough to fill a small spoon'.

Baudelaire, however, made various reservations. 'Hashish', he conceded in *Paradis Artificiels*, 'shows to a man nothing but himself'; and it is not a risk that everyone will take, or, if he takes it, finds he can endure. Among visitors to the Hôtel Lauzun came Balzac and Ernest Meissonier; and, whereas the great novelist, tempted to accept the pernicious sweetmeat, was fascinated, 'and listened and asked questions with an amusing attentiveness and curiosity', he was shocked by the 'notion of

---

* 'Opium is a peaceful seducer; hashish is a disorderly demon'; *Paradis Artificiels*, translated by Norman Cameron, 1950. On Coleridge it had the same effect. He wished, he said, 'like Vishnu to float . . . along an infinite ocean cradled in the flower of the Lotus, and wake once in a million years just to know that I was going to sleep a million years more'.

Baudelaire's caricature of himself under the influence of hashish, 'the drug that shows to a man nothing but himself'.

letting his thoughts pass beyond his own control . . . His inner conflict between his almost childish eagerness for knowledge and his loathing of self-surrender, was revealed on his expressive countenance', until his love of human dignity had won the day and he had decided that he must refuse. The popular artist, on the other hand, agreed to try the drug, which, no doubt, he thought, would bring out his splendid creative gifts, but was sharply disappointed to find himself wandering through a labyrinth of immense geometric parterres. 'I might have been in one of Le Nôtre's gardens!' he disgustedly exclaimed.

So far as we can now judge, none of the adventurous Haschisins did himself inoperable harm. Syphilis then was still the great adversary that carried off so many artists; and one may forget that, until the end of the Second World War, drug-addiction and its commercial exploitation had yet to become a major public problem. At Oxford, in 1924 and 1925, though we practised many other forms of self-indulgence, among my fellow undergraduates I cannot remember encountering an addict; and my few tentative experiments with drugs were reserved for later life. The oddest and the most disturbing was made about 1958, when, at a rather raffish New York evening party, the guests were offered a mixture of heroin and cocaine (picturesquely renamed 'hyacinth' and 'crocus') which we inhaled from little wooden spoons; and, besides completely abolishing my sense of time, it eliminated the smallest trace of boredom or fatigue, so that I spent nearly the whole night engaged in a sensible and decorous conversation with an English woman friend, whom I liked but neither loved nor particularly admired.

During a slightly earlier stage of my life, I had been invited to smoke opium at a pre-war dinner-party in Peking, where my host, a musician and himself an opium-lover, kindly acted as my guide. The procedure had a ceremonious charm. First, the raw opium was cooked, crackling and bubbling over a small flame, to which the pipe's bowl, a circular metal disc, must then be kept carefully applied; and I was told to breathe in constantly and regularly, 'like a child', said my experienced host, 'sucking at its mother's breast'. Clearly this ritual, which necessitated fixing one's eyes on a single brilliant point of light, while gazing down the pipe's long polished stem, had a mild hypnotic influence. I smoked only a few pipes and left the

huge Victorian brass bed, on which, overlooked by an array of tin alarm-clocks and other odd apparatus of a Chinese dining-room, I had been invited to recline, feeling calm and content, but no more intoxicated or illuminated than if I had smoked a strong Churchillian cigar. Certainly I felt no worse; the evils of the habit, Chinese acquaintances assured me, were often considerably exaggerated, provided the opium employed was pure, contained no dross scraped out of previous pipes, but came straight from the vast poppy-fields that, in those days, stretched beyond the Great Wall. The habit developed very slowly; and a general carelessness and lassitude, which admittedly might have disastrous results, sometimes accompanied by constipation and even sexual impotence, were frequently among its deadliest symptoms.

My last experience of the effect of drugs was both accidental and ridiculous. Ten or fifteen years ago, when I had attempted to cross a glazed roof on some ill-advised domestic errand, I heard the horrid sound of cracking glass, felt my foothold giving way and, with the sensation of a letter being mailed, shot down into the room below. It was a fairly heavy fall, and, as I lay immobile on the floor, a friendly doctor stood over me and began a good-natured inquisition. He thought, he said, that I might have suffered 'cerebral damage'; and, by way of testing my wits, he suggested that I should now repeat the names of the last five British Prime Ministers – a task, I had to confess, of which, whatever my state of mind, I should have been utterly incapable. After some further brief examinations, he therefore bade me goodbye, but left behind him a few large brown pills that he recommended I should take if I had a painful, restless night.

My night was undisturbed; but I am always interested in unknown pills, and maybe I exceeded the proper dose; for next day I found that my vision of existence had undergone a dazzling change. I believe that the pills' basis may conceivably have been morphine, which my dictionary describes as an 'alkaloid principle of opium . . . popularly called "morphia" '. That morning I entered a new world, or a world with which I was already familiar, but now marvellously transmogrified. Here scenes and objects that had once been commonplace had acquired an extraordinary fascination. I looked forward eagerly to the coming day and all the visual splendours that it promised – in the glorious red of an omnibus and the

Piranesian flight of steps that would lead me down to the station-platform whence an eagle-swift train would waft me to my Fleet Street office.

In fact, I had achieved a degree of euphoria, indistinguishable from true happiness, that, although it slowly faded and declined, had lasted, so far as I can recollect, some two or three delightful hours. Such, no doubt, was the Artificial Paradise Baudelaire and his fellow Haschisins claimed to have conquered at a stroke, but from which the addict, having set foot there, is eventually expelled. I have never entered that paradise again; during my absence, a well-wisher decided to destroy my pills. Nor do I regret their loss; but it was an experience worth having. I am glad to have seen a temporarily transfigured world, and mounted a London omnibus so superbly coloured and majestic that it resembled a 'Chariot of fire' in one of Blake's Prophetic Books.

Voyages of Discovery

I N my early childhood, if my spirits were low, I was often told to 'count
my blessings' – advice that, between 1905 and 1914, as the eldest son of
a fairly prosperous middle-class English family, I did not find it hard
to follow. Since those far-off days it has become increasingly difficult, now
that the world itself is threatened with atomic devastation, and so many
fields of human happiness are constantly invaded and destroyed. Yet,
while some have vanished or are fast vanishing, others have been opened
up; and the preliminary steps towards such a discovery were first taken
over two hundred years ago by an intrepid Frenchman named Alexandre
Charles. He was not the earliest astronaut to leave the surface of the globe;
only a month earlier, Pilâtre de Rozier and his friend, the marquis
d'Arlandes, had enjoyed the first free flight towards the heavens. But their
ascent had lasted less than half-an-hour; and the balloon that carried them
was lifted by hot air, and therefore quite unsuited to a lengthy passage.
Charles, on the other hand, and his companion Robert, whose immense
yellow-and-ochre balloon contained hydrogen, once they had risen from
the Gardens of the Tuileries floated off westwards across open country,
pursued on horseback at breakneck speed by two enthusiastic noblemen,
the duc de Chartres and the duc de FitzJames, and as, some forty
kilometres beyond Paris, Charles began his descent, by peasants running
through the fields 'like children chasing a butterfly', he wrote.

After a successful landing, the chief astronaut decided on a second
venture, abandoned Robert in order to lighten his load, and, having re-
entered the gondola that hung beneath the balloon – a rococo *coquillage*
embellished with golden wings, a royal crown and *fleurs-de-lis* – rose this

time, according to his own eloquent narrative, about two miles above the earth. Nothing, he thought, could ever equal the splendid 'moment of hilarity' he had experienced when his enormous craft again smoothly cleared the ground; and now he had an even deeper and more entrancing satisfaction:

> 'The cold was sharp and dry, but not at all unbearable. I could then examine . . . my sensations in complete tranquillity . . . I stood up in the middle of the gondola, and lost myself in the spectacle offered by the immensity of the horizon.'

He felt, we learn, a sense of almost mystical happiness, of 'inexpressible delight', and 'an ecstasy of contemplation' he had never known before:

> 'No human being, I reflected , has yet penetrated these solitudes; man's voice has never been heard here, and I struck the air with a few sounds as if to stir the silence all around me. The calm, the gathering darkness, that immensity in the midst of which I was floating. All this gripped my soul . . .'*

Charles, in fact, seems to have discovered a totally new form of happiness; and this account of his emotions above the earth may be compared with Rousseau's rediscovery of happiness, in 1765, beside the Lac de Bienne. But, during the present period, a friend, who has passed many years flying American fighter-planes, informs me that Charles's romantic sensations are sometimes shared by modern airmen, and that he himself has felt them more than once, for example, when, having flown seven hundred miles to attend the funeral of a companion killed in a flying accident, he climbed to thirty-five thousand feet, and there the rapture Charles so well conveyed took complete possession of his mind.† Night had fallen; viewed from that altitude, the sky was a deep blue-black, with a huge full moon and a host of stars that looked extraordinarily large and bright. The funeral had

---

* Charles Coulston Gillispie: for a detailed account of Charles's adventures, see *The Montgolfier Brothers and the Invention of Aviation*, 1983.

† At an altitude of more than two miles, this state of mind, which is named *hypoxia*, and involves a heightened sense of one's true identity and a feeling of union with Nature, is said to be the general experience of flyers.

saddened him; it had seemed a dull, unmeaning ceremony. But now that he had reached 'the edge of space' he had a marvellous sense of solitude; and, determined he must pay his dead friend homage, he performed a succession of great looping manoeuvres, called 'barrel-rolls', 'aileron rolls' and 'lazy eights'.

Thus, although modern life frequently destroys happiness, or provides vulgar marketable substitutes, its pursuers need not yet lose hope. New experiences may still await us. I have already quoted Ruskin's announcement that seeing was 'the noblest thing' a soul could do; and during the last hundred years, even the last three or four decades, our range of vision has been extraordinarily enlarged. Sights that would have fascinated, though perhaps alarmed and disturbed, Ruskin are constantly presented to us on the television-screen. We can follow the flight of a humming-bird, peer down into the vividly coloured labyrinth of a Caribbean coral-reef, study the strange inhabitants of an Eastern rain-forest, or, high above the gloomy, sodden forest-floor, visit the huge aerial plateau of sunlit leaves and flowers that stretches far away across the jungle. One night, as the ship on which I was then travelling towards Japan approached a distant, dusky coast-line, a faint but exquisite fragrance crept along the deck, the scent, I was told, of innumerable blossoms that, because they spring only amid the loftiest branches, very few botanists had ever seen.

Today, thanks to modern climbing-equipment and an adventurous use of the camera, those same flowers, like the vast population of beasts and birds and insects who pass their whole lives immediately beneath the sky, have been examined and recorded.* Yet, although our knowledge of the natural world has so remarkably increased, the workings of Nature itself have grown more and more mysterious. Between eighteenth-century poets, William Collins, James Thomson, John Dyer, Thomas Gray, and the natural scenes they described, there was still a strong admiring sympathy; Nature they regarded as 'greatly charming'; he knew of 'no

---

* Rope-climbing techniques were first employed in the jungle not many years ago; and from David Attenborough's richly instructive and rightly popular book *The Living Planet* we learn that an earlier botanist, anxious to catalogue the forest trees of Borneo, was obliged to train a monkey, which, having climbed a tree he pointed out, would pick and throw down its leaves and flowers.

subject', wrote Thomson in his preface to his famous work *The Seasons*, 'more elevating, more amusing; more ready to awake . . . the philosophic reflection, and moral sentiment . . . Where can we meet with such variety, such beauty, such magnificence?' At the same period, connoisseurs of painting would often carry around an ingenious apparatus called a 'Claude Glass' that enabled them, while they contemplated a landscape, to distinguish its resemblance to a classic work of art; and the poet carried in his mind a somewhat similar device that helped him bring out the moral and philosophical aspects of the scene that met his eyes.

Much less comforting is the point of view of the twentieth-century spectator, now that the strangeness and wildness of the natural world seem to increase with every discovery we make. Until Charles Darwin had entered the field, for example, the methods of propagation and self-preservation that certain flowers and insects employ were still unknown to modern scientists. Who could have guessed, for example, that some South-American orchids, in order to attract the fly they need to transfer their pollen, had developed a system of mimicry so fantastically elaborate that it defied even a Darwinian explanation – sometimes representing themselves as female insects to attract a wandering male; sometimes swaying like a swarm of bees which the real bee may be tempted to attack; or, now and then, alluring a victim by means of a female fragrance they exude and, once it has entered the labyrinth, intoxicating it by a liquid they distil,* so that the drunken insect may lose its balance and waywardly brush its wings against a hidden stem where a store of precious pollinea awaits collection?

The argument, dear to eighteenth-century sermonists, that the ingenious design of the universe reveals the existence of a benevolent Creator,† may lead in more than one direction. Might we not also suspect that it was the masterpiece of a sublimely eccentric Intelligence which revelled in its own complexity? Such was Victor Hugo's opinion. His relationship with

---

* The orchid pollinated by drunken bees is named *Stanhopea Wardii*. See Alice Skelsey: *Orchids*, 1979.

† The chief English advocate of the so-called 'Argument from Design' was William Paley (1743–1805), whose *Evidences of Christianity*, published in 1794, Sir Timothy Shelley often recommended to his disbelieving son Percy Bysshe. The 'Argument' was strongly opposed both by Kant and by Hume.

the Creator was always engagingly personal; and on the verge of death he remarked to a young disciple that he would very soon be meeting God; and 'what a magnificent occasion that would be!' He often though of it, and was already preparing his speech. Meanwhile, at an earlier stage of his life, he had gone so far as to reproach the Creator with the bizarre diversity of his creation, in which humming-birds, flowers and rainbows were accompanied by the presence of huge monstrous reptiles; and he occasionally wondered if God, though like himself a great poet, did not, at certain moments, show a curious lack of good taste.* But then, he concluded, some excuses should probably be made for the Universal Genius!

Although we may not share Victor Hugo's views, we must still admit that, the more we know of creation, the more difficult it becomes to reconcile it with any idea, human or divine, of harmony and order. Yet, whatever the effect of a new discovery may be, discovering itself remains a happy exercise. Alexandre Charles, in his balloon 'about two miles above the earth', felt not merely scientific satisfaction but a sense of 'inexpressible delight'; and something of the same delight must be enjoyed by the earth-bound seeker after knowledge when he suddenly reaps his reward – by a botanist, for example, in the old days of famous plant-hunters, while they were still allowed to explore Asiatic terrains that today are prohibited 'military zones', should he happen to cross a Himalayan range and see far below him a whole valley filled with unknown trees and flowers. Archaeologists, too, are, now and then, equally fortunate; and I recollect my old friend Seton Lloyd describing, many years ago, such an especially memorable occasion.† As he excavated a small Sumerian shrine, he noticed that the knife of an elderly workman, told to scrape a clay floor, had inadvertently broken through the surface and opened a large cavity beneath. Having struck a match, Seton gazed down into the gulf, and there confronted the unbroken alabaster votive statue of an ancient Sumerian citizen, his hands folded in prayer on his naked chest, his solemn big-nosed

* *'Moi, je n'exige pas que Dieu toujours s'observe,*
  Il faut bien tolérer quelques excès de verve
  Chez un si grand poète, et ne point se fâcher . . .
  C'est son humeur à lui d'être de mauvais goût'
† It is well described in his extremely interesting book, *Mesopotamia: Excavations in Sumerian Sites*, 1936.

countenance framed in black shoulder-length curls and long black densely corrugated beard. But the most impressive feature of the face that looked up at him were its enormous globular eyes, inlaid with lapis lazuli and polished bone, on which the sun now gleamed 'for the first time in five thousand years.'*

My own ambition to become an archaeologist, encouraged by a chance meeting with the renowned Sir Leonard Woolley, the great discoverer of Ur, was presently extinguished both by my sad failure to win an academic degree and by the lack of a small private income that, Sir Leonard said, a young archaeologist usually required. In my youth, however, I had a single modest *trouvaille*, when, walking over the Chilterns, near a prehistoric barrow, I happened to kick down a molehill and unearthed a carefully-pierced wolf's tooth that an expert at the British Museum recognised as having originally hung in a Stone Age hunter's necklace. Otherwise the gift of 'Serendipity' – the word Horace Walpole coined to describe a mysterious aptitude for making unexpected, if sometimes useless, finds – has very seldom come my way. After discovering the wolf's tooth, nevertheless, I had a single stroke of luck that, although itself even more insignificant, caused me momentary delight. Shown a small wooden casket, a beautiful piece of work that had clearly come from an early-nineteenth-century dressing-table and contained many ingenious parti-tions, I suggested that, if only we could find the right place, it must enclose a secret drawer, and then, fumbling around, happened to alight upon the hidden spring. Behind the minute panel that obediently leapt open lay a store of little three-penny pieces that carried King William IV's head, and were still as delicate and brightly polished as if they had just been issued from the Mint.

Among discoveries, great and small, scientific, imaginative, phantasmago-ric, that have aided the pursuit of happiness, self-discovery must take a place. The maxim 'Know Thyself', which Montaigne had inscribed on his ceiling, has an universal application; and any honest autobiography should give us an account not only of the discoveries a man has made about

---

* Crushed beneath lay another dozen votive statues, male and female, now known collectively as 'the 'Tell Asmara hoard'.

himself but of the circumstances in which he made them. For Montaigne, an unusually well-balanced character, they were always an absorbing subject. Like the learned English physician and master of poetic prose, Sir Thomas Browne, he believed that Man was among the strangest phenomena the natural world could show, and deserved as much study: 'I could never content my contemplation', he wrote in *Religio Medici*, 'with those general pieces of wonder, the Flux and Reflux of the Sea, the increase of Nile, the converse of the Needle to the North . . . We carry with us the wonders we seek without us: there is all Africa and her prodigies in us . . .; since bold and adventurous' Man was a 'great and true Amphibian . . . disposed to live . . . in divided and distinguished worlds', both in the spirit and in ordinary sensuous existence, and in both to flourish and evolve.

Thus introspection, which, if wrongly and self-destructively employed, becomes an unending source of misery, may also, as Montaigne found, once we have explored the Africa we carry around within ourselves, help us to establish a reasonable degree of happiness. Here we are assisted by the discoveries we make; a life from which an ability to discover was absent would indeed be dark and wretched. The process begins at a very early age, usually the moment we have learned that we can read; and I recollect the time, and even the exact place, at which for me this miracle occurred – lying on the tiled floor of my parents' dining room, as I turned the pages of a yellow-clad magazine, and saw the long pageant of a continuous narrative unfolding dramatically beneath my eyes. I cannot date this adventure exactly; but it must, I think, have not been very long after my father had carried me out of the house to observe a luminous blur called Halley's Comet* floating rather low down in the heavens; and just before, through a neighbour's telescope I had been shown the Rings of Saturn and the mysterious Mountains of the Moon, on which, I was told to notice, the dawn was then breaking.

All these were memorable experiences; but the discovery that I could read was evidently the most decisive, for it set me out on a journey of exploration that has continued ever since, and, I hope, will end only with my life. Meanwhile, I am so addicted to the printed word that, if I am

* Named after the astronomer Esmond Halley (1656–1742), it reappears, as it did recently, every seventy-eight years.

temporarily deprived of books, I find myself eagerly studying newspaper advertisements or the inscriptions plastered around medicine-bottles. At the same time, to the happiness that reading brought me, I added the joy of enlarging my vision of the world in which I lived, for example, by scrutinising the pictures, often late-Victorian reproductions of the Italian masters, Botticelli, Carpaccio and Gozzoli, that my parents hung upon their walls. These works themselves, and the inexplicable details the artist had sometimes chosen to portray, aroused an avid curiosity. 'Children', observed John Locke, 'are travellers newly arrived in a strange country'; and 'for a child', wrote Baudelaire in his famous essay on the draughtsman Constantin Guys, 'everything is new . . . nothing bears a more striking resemblance to what is called inspiration than the joy with which forms and colours are absorbed by the child'; while Coleridge, whose *Biographia Literaria* Baudelaire seems unlikely to have read, agreed that 'to carry on the feelings of childhood into the power of manhood; to combine the child's sense of wonder and novelty with the appearances which every day had . . . rendered familiar . . . is the character and privilege of genius'.

Still closer was the link that Wordsworth thought he could distinguish between his rapturous experiences as a child and his evolution as a poet; and, if *The Prelude* is much the most moving account of an imaginative childhood yet written in the English language, it is because, to the various strains of youthful feeling that had helped to make him what he was, he added its 'terrors, pains and early miseries' and 'the impressive influence of Fear'. Nature, which delighted, also sometimes terrified him, and a sense of 'visionary dreariness', of 'want and horror'* would temporarily weigh him down. The idea of childhood as the happiest period of man's life, of course, is an adult fiction. Yet there seems no doubt that keen joy and profound wretchedness, eager expectation and crushing disappointment, are then more acutely contrasted than at any other period. But, 'fostered alike by beauty and by fear', it is still, in Wordsworth's term, 'the seed-time of the soul', the point at which our voyage of discovery begins. Not until the poet himself had halted its progress, and set about systematising and moralising his observations, did his genius at last decline.

* 'Another time in a lowering and sad evening . . . a certain want and horror fell upon me, beyond imagination' – Thomas Traherne (1637–74); *Centuries of Meditations*.

13

The Philosopher's Garden

EPICURUS, the philosopher once described by La Fontaine as 'the noblest of Greek spirits', and the adjective 'epicurean', which his name presently inspired, seem to have developed a somewhat derogatory significance many years before the birth of Christ. Thus the pleasure-loving poet Horace, whose sybaritic life and growing corpulence amused both his literary patron Maecenas and his sovereign the Emperor Augustus, tells a friend in one of his *Epistles* that he is now becoming sleek and fat – '*Epicuri de grege porcum*', a hog from Epicurus' stye – and advises him to follow the philosopher's example, to take no thought of the morrow, and conduct his personal life as if the next day might prove to be his last.*

Yet Epicurus, who entered the world in 341 BC and left it in 270, was a deeply serious philosopher and attracted no less serious students. A native of Samos, after 306 he had made his home in Athens, where he purchased a large and magnificent garden in which, as he walked, he lectured to his school. The greatest good, he informed them, was happiness; and, whereas the Stoics, whose founder was Zeno of Samos, asserted that virtue should be cultivated for its own sake, Epicurus, a thorough-going Pragmatist, declared that, although to live happily one must also live wisely and well, pleasure itself was 'the beginning and end of the blessed life'; and that 'beauty, virtue and the like' were to be valued only 'if they produced pleasure; and if they did not, we must bid them goodbye'.

---

* Plato had said that the luxurious citizens of Akragas, called by Pindar 'the loveliest city of mortals', built as though they dismissed the thought of death, and dined as if they assumed that their next dinner-party would be the last they might enjoy.

Epicurus' interpretation of pleasure, on the other hand, was by no means primarily physical. What he sought, and advised his followers to seek, was a steadfast quietude of mind, a state he entitled *ataraxia*, which would both protect them against the fear of death and dispel a superstitious terror of the Gods, whose existence he did not deny, but whom he assumed to be completely detached from, and sublimely indifferent to, the affairs of mankind.* A similarly estimable attribute he called *galené*, an ability to remain calm even in the centre of a storm. But there was nothing unduly passive or soporific about the gospel that he preached. It demanded constant effort. 'Friendship and affection dance around the world', he said in one of his rare published dicta, reminding us that, to enjoy happiness, we must deliberately exert ourselves.

For the benefit of his followers, in whom he inspired a keen personal attachment, Epicurus is reputed to have written some three hundred books and a long series of letters, which, it is thought, may perhaps in certain respects have slightly resembled the *Epistles* of St. Paul. Few have been preserved. More fortunate was his predecessor Aristotle, a citizen of Macedonia, born in 384 BC, whose teachings survived to instruct the Middle Ages, and who devoted the whole first volume of his *Nicomachean Ethics* to the theme of 'human welfare or Happiness', which he 'found to consist in the active exercise of . . . the virtues of man's nature'. Based apparently on his lecture-notes, the *Ethics* are not an immediately attractive work; and Thomas Gray complained that Aristotle was 'the hardest author by far I ever meddled with . . . He has a dry conciseness that makes one imagine one is perusing a table of contents rather than a book; it tastes for all the world like chopped hay . . .'

Yet his central message is strongly and consistently maintained. Happiness, Aristotle believed, 'is not a product of action', but itself a form of activity, a mode of life that depends on the employment of pure reason. The happy man is one who 'lives well', or 'does well'; for, whereas the majority of mankind seek enjoyment from confused and conflicting sources, the votary of what is noble naturally finds his pleasure in actions that conform to virtue; and, since such actions are always essentially pleasurable, he requires no other joy. Happiness, therefore, is not a by-

---

* The separateness and indifference of the Gods is also described by two famous poets, Lucretius in *De Rerum Natura* and Tennyson in *The Lotos-Eaters*.

product of mere worldly good fortune. It is in itself 'a thing honoured and perfect . . . the great principle or starting point' from which all that is best in human life derives, and therefore, 'the supreme end and aim of conduct'.

Across the centuries we can distinguish an obvious link between the Macedonian philosopher and the first President of the United States, from whose Inaugural Address I have already quoted; and, since Washington's day, the true nature of happiness and its connection with virtue have provoked unending arguments. On these debates social changes have evidently had some effect. In England, during the second half of the eighteenth century, while France had her Voltairean Enlightenment, Britain's educated citizens believed that they inhabited a continuously changing and improving world. Georgian London was thought to resemble Antonine Rome; never had intellectual standards been so high, or personal habits more refined. The metropolis itself, since Hogarth painted it, had become a far cleaner and quieter place. There was less crime and drunkenness – legislation had reduced gin-drinking; and its streets were better paved and better lighted. 'The present age', Lord Chesterfield informed his contemporaries, 'has . . . the honour and pleasure of being extremely well with me'.

During the mid-nineteenth century, however, although Victorians were rightly pleased with their material progress, a shade of anxiety and doubt, accompanied by fears of some impending revolutionary upheaval, shared by writers otherwise as far apart as Ruskin, Matthew Arnold and Disraeli, often underlay their pride; and such questions as whether a man should expect happiness, or, indeed, deserved to be happy, became particularly numerous. The period's most gifted and argumentative prose-writers were all to some extent concerned with them. Ruskin came near to happiness by the use he made of his eyes and his knowledge of, and devotion to, the visual arts, but despaired of it in his emotional life; Carlyle sternly rejected it as an aim; and his friend John Stuart Mill declared, like Aristotle, that virtue was 'happiness in its highest form' and seems to have found a measure of personal contentment in his long devoted relationship with Mrs Taylor, a learned, high-minded lady, by the Carlyles significantly nicknamed 'Platonica', adding nevertheless: 'Ask yourself whether you are happy and you cease to be so', just as Jane Carlyle had compared

happiness with a spirit that, if one mentioned its name, was apt immediately to disappear. Of the later Victorians, Robert Louis Stevenson, a man for whom, both in his personal and in his literary character, Henry James felt a particularly deep affection, seems to have followed Joseph Joubert's lead. He, too, asserted that life was a duty of which we should do all we can to make a pleasure, but a duty, that we consistently neglect and underrate more than we do almost any other obligation.

Today, as guides to the Happy Life, philosophers are rivalled, and have been to some extent replaced, by psychologists and social moralists; while modern journalists, English and French, sometimes produce an enlivening 'middle' on the subject. I have here, for instance, an essay by a thoughtful woman writer, once cut from the pages of the popular press, in which she explains her view of what constitutes happiness, and how it may most simply be achieved. She does not belong to the Aristotelian school, 'because [she reminds us] happiness can't be bought, organised, bequeathed or even earned. You can be worthy, pious, forever . . . giving old crusts to starving birds . . . and remain as sad as sin . . . Happiness you've got to be susceptible to. You've got to like yourself enough to be prepared to indulge in it . . . when it suddenly rears up . . .' It is not a right, but a quality we 'unearth in ourselves' and that depends on our ability to seize, cherish and enjoy the pleasures of the passing moment.*

Today, psychiatrists, Freudian or Jungian, also offer us their advice in print; and among the popular biographies and semi-pornographic romances that crowd a modern bookshop's shelves, one finds numerous admonitory publications, such as a slim best-seller that recently came my way, entitled *How to be your Own Best Friend*, subtitled *A Conversation with two Psychoanalysts*, named Newman and Berkowitz, who, we read, 'have already helped thousands of people to lead more rewarding lives'. In the entourage of the rich and powerful, I have been told, a salaried analyst sometimes occupies much the same position as an alchemist or soothsayer used often to hold in the court of a European sovereign or grandee, and that the great executive may frequently consult him before undertaking some momentous move. The booklet I have mentioned seems to be

* Lynda Lee-Potter, *Daily Mail*, 15 February 1984.

addressed to a somewhat less exigent section of society, to ordinary people asking the ordinary questions of modern life, but still wanting an adequate reply. Questions of this kind, the two analysts believe, are growing more and more numerous. 'When Thoreau remarked', they write in their prefatory chapter, 'that most men live lives of quiet desperation, he could not have foreseen how noisy that desperation would become . . . Modern man . . . does not suffer in silence. Our malaise is articulate . . . Resignation is not for us; if we are unhappy, we feel cheated, displaced, left out . . .'

The modern world, they observe, offers us an immense variety of diversions; but none seems to provide the escape-route that their patients need. And may not this, they enquire, be due to the fact that 'too many people have just not mastered the art of being happy?' For happiness, they contend, is certainly an art we can learn; and a multitude of sufferers, who 'go to a lot of trouble to learn French or physics or scuba diving', lack the patience or clear-sightedness to set about its acquisition, a feat they can only accomplish by learning to look into, and thus assume a responsible attitude towards, themselves. They should try their hardest to 'operate' their own characters just as they have discovered how to drive a motor-car, and thus at last become their own best friends.

In the advice they give, readers will soon notice, Newman and Berkowitz make few references either to religious faith or to the lasting happiness we find in imaginative art. Nor, although, as analysts, they believe that 'analysis is a great tool of liberation', and when the first patient lay down on the couch, it was a 'truly giant step for mankind', they agree that, once a sufferer has left the couch, there are many problems he may have failed to solve; while Freudian terms are, no doubt deliberately, avoided. I have mentioned the book here because it represents, like some of Epicurus' sayings, a completely pragmatic approach to the problems that it poses. In modern commercial society, the art of happiness can be learned without much more difficulty than the management of an efficient twentieth-century vehicle.

A similarly euphoric little book, clearly addressed to somewhat more simple-minded readers, but also popular on airport bookshelves, is Dr Norman Vincent Peale's *Positive Thoughts for the Day*, an ambitious compilation of '366 upbeat and positive thoughts, one for every day in the year', which he hopes that his converts will keep readily available on a desk

or on a bedside table, or in the kitchen, 'or perhaps have a copy in each place'. The author has already published thirteen manuals of the same kind, which include, with two collaborators' assistance, *The Art of Real Happiness*; and each records his own thoughts on a variety of elevating topics. He suggests that we should tear them from the page, inscribe them on a card, and preserve them in a shirt-pocket. 'Putting the cards into the pocket means putting the quotations over the heart, thus emphasizing the emotional factor.' There they may have many daily uses: 'While driving your car, if you become annoyed . . . by another driver, instead of reacting in kind – send up a sincere prayer for him . . . Perhaps your prayer may reach his problem. One thing is sure; it will reach you . . .'

Pocket-moralists will continue to flourish so long as they can find an audience. But, since in 1903 George Edward Moore published his *Principia Ethica*, few genuine philosophers have considered the subject of happiness and its emotional and intellectual value. Bertrand Russell's treatise on *The Conquest of Happiness*, which appeared in 1930, did not attract, as *Principia* had done, a group of enthusiastic sympathisers. It is, even his votaries confess, one of his least stimulating books. On philosophic and mathematical questions, those who themselves can climb to the same heights assure us, he wrote brilliantly lucid prose; but here his style has a kind of dry, angular didacticism that constantly exasperates the reader. His opinions, too, social and political alike, are sometimes curiously perverse. He introduces and dismisses subjects with an air of irritable self-assurance, knocks a contradictory statement down and brusquely pushes it aside. In the early 1930s he was still a staunch supporter of the Russian Revolution;* and, when he discusses happiness and where it may most often be found, he announces that

> the intelligent young at the present day are probably happier . . . in Russia than anywhere else in the world. They have there a new world to create . . . The old have been executed, starved, exiled, or in some way disinfected, so that they cannot, as in every Western country, compel the young to choose between doing harm and doing nothing.

* Lenin, he wrote, was 'the supreme type' of the statesman who has directed his whole life to producing order out of chaos.

There is an unpleasant unction about Russell's use of words 'otherwise disinfected' that recalls a speech by Robespierre, Desmoulins or Saint-Just. Like many protagonists of the French Revolution, Russell had had an aristocratic origin; the Russells, kinsmen of the Duke of Bedford, belonged to a rich and important clan that had played a large progressive part in the history of Great Britain; and he combined a patrician intransigence with all the intellectual arrogance of a highly gifted man. Thus, having been born among the rich, he felt entitled to despise them as a class. Today, he informs us, the rich man 'never reads. If he is creating a picture gallery, he relies upon experts to choose his pictures; the pleasure he derives from them is not the pleasure of looking at them, but the pleasure of depriving some other rich man from having them', though 'in regard to music, if he happens to be a Jew, he may have a genuine appreciation . . .'

Russell's own sensitiveness to Beauty as a source of happiness appears to have been remarkably restricted. He valued love, however, 'because it enhances the best pleasures . . . A man who has never enjoyed beautiful things in the company of a woman whom he loved has not experienced to the full the magic power of which such things are capable'. Otherwise, his instructions for the conquest of happiness are often very largely negative; he gives a long list of the states of mind we should carefully avoid – competitiveness, boredom, fatigue, envy, the sense of sin, persecution mania, fear of public opinion – all weaknesses he castigates at considerable length.

Then, having enumerated the *Causes of Unhappiness*, he devotes the second half of his book to 'considering the happy man' and heads his first chapter with the poignant question 'Is happiness still possible?' to which he answers that, given the right circumstances and some smattering of common sense, it is certainly within our reach. 'The happy life', he echoes Aristotle, is 'to an extraordinary extent' indistinguishable from the good life. It is also a quiet life, as the records of many great men show. 'The happy man', he concludes, 'is the man who lives objectively, who has free affections and wide interests', and is untroubled by the fears of death thanks to his instinctive sense of union with the natural world at large. Russell 'wrote as a hedonist', he said; and the asset he valued most, though I am not sure he ever achieved it himself, was the quality that the Greeks called *ataraxia*, the steadfast quietude of mind Epicurus had once recommended while he walked round his Athenian garden.

14

A New Athens

THE first thirteen years of the twentieth century were not one of those enlightened epochs in which we sometimes wish that we had lived ourselves; nor do modern social historians give us a very pleasant picture of the age. Yet for those who at the time were already grown up but still comparatively young, it was a period of hope and promise; and in his autobiography Leonard Woolf has described how, on his return to England from Ceylon, the European scene delighted him. Whereas since the Second World War, he points out, we have learned to live 'more or less contentedly' beneath the shadow of some huge impending disaster, he then felt a general sense of security, accompanied by a 'growing belief that it was a supremely good thing for people to be communally and individually happy'.

Both in London and in Cambridge, Woolf had an extremely kind reception. His old university was full of good friends; and, although that part of the English literary landscape we now call 'Bloomsbury' had not yet definitely taken shape, he again met and admired Virginia and Vanessa Stephen, both beautiful in their strange Pre-Raphaelite way, and both, he saw, extremely talented. They were the feminine stars of a no less gifted society; and around them gathered such rising young intellectuals as Roger Fry, Clive Bell, whom Vanessa married, Lytton Strachey, Desmond Mc-Carthy and Maynard Keynes. Their guide through life was the philosopher George Edward Moore, author of *Principia Ethica*, which they all first read at Cambridge and had become their layman's gospel. Moore's message made an immediate appeal to the young. 'By far the most valuable things, which we know or can imagine', he assured his followers, 'are certain states

of consciousness, which may be rightly described as the pleasures of human intercourse and the enjoyment of beautiful objects . . . It is only for the sake of these things . . . that any-one can be justified in performing any public or private duty . . . They are the *raison d'être* of virtue . . .' This message was simple and moving enough; but Moore had also a passion for exactitude; and '*Exactly* what do you mean by that?' he would often demand with a curious sidelong movement of his head.*

The influence of *Principia Ethica* on the citizens of the Bloomsburian world was evidently strong and far-reaching; for not only did it encourage their love of art, but it glorified their cult of friendship. Around Virginia Woolf and her associates a great deal of academic rubbish has recently been piled up. They were not a 'school', a 'movement', a '*cénacle*', so much as a group of close friends, who, except for Roger Fry and the Misses Stephen, had originally met and talked at Cambridge, and in London still found one another's conversation and companionship highly stimulating and enjoyable. Moore had emphasised the importance of the personal affections, which in the scale of human values, his disciple the economist Maynard Keynes declared, should always come 'a long way first'; and, though they might sometimes disagree and, since they were most of them somewhat malicious conversationalists, poke rather acid fun at an old friend's private foibles, friends they remained throughout their adult lives. It was their passion for the truth, natural communicativeness, desire to establish a 'mental intimacy' with those they knew and loved – an idea to be effective *must* be shared, they thought – that gave them their peculiar distinction.

Unluckily the Bloomsburians had no Boswell; but, in her reminiscences,† Frances Partridge, an engaging youthful member of the group, beloved by Ralph Partridge who was himself beloved by Lytton Strachey, recorded the remarkable variety of subjects that they enjoyed discussing, and that, both in bed and at breakfast the next day, might vary from such

* See *The Bloomsbury Group: A study of E.M. Forster, Lytton Strachey, Virginia Woolf, and their Circle*, J.K. Johnstone, 1954.
† *Memories*, 1981.

human problems as the origins of sentimentality and 'modesty about facts' to interesting literary questions – had Lady Ashburton really been Carlyle's mistress? – and, a little later, might lead to 'an interesting argument' on logic, provoked by Bertrand Russell's new book, which Frances at the time was reading. Similarly, Roger Fry would hold up a dinner-party while he read aloud from his renderings of Mallarmé's poems, and – 'with magnificent reverberations', Virginia Woolf said – describe the nature of the Symbolist poet's genius. Yet the tone of these colloquies, however erudite their theme, was always spontaneous and enthusiastic rather than dogmatic. They talked as readily and, indeed, as volubly as their predecessors had done during the great days of the French Enlightenment; and Clive Bell, the group's most vocal member, had acquired the precious gift of persuading his guests, when they dined with him at his flat above Gordon Square, that, thanks to their presence, and the learning and wit they displayed, this was an occasion some of the most distinguished talkers of the past would have been flattered to attend.

'. . . Happiness', wrote Leonard Woolf in 1964, 'is politically now a dirty word'; but the Bloomsburians, inspired by Moore, were certainly devoted to the quest. For only one of them, Virginia Woolf, did it prove almost insuperably difficult. From the threat of madness she would never long escape; and her physical attitude towards the world betrayed the sufferings of her mind. 'She had,' writes Frances Partridge, an 'agonised tautness . . . The way she held herself, turned her head or smoked a cigarette struck one as awkward even while it charmed . . .' In her vicinity one felt an electric current circulating; and few of her younger visitors were always completely at their ease. Vanessa Bell, on the other hand, charmed and reassured while Virginia troubled and perplexed. She seemed a happy woman; and her dearest companions – her husband, the euphoric Clive, her long-devoted lover, Roger Fry, and her fellow painter Duncan Grant with whom she spent her last years – were all prolific and argumentative characters.

Stendhal's definitions of happiness as the offspring of 'love + work' was a maxim that the Bloomsburian group appear to have put successfully into practice. Their personal and their professional lives, their friendships and their love affairs, were very often closely linked; and in some ways the

records of their communal life may impress us more than many of the works they left behind them. Roger Fry was a fascinating, highly gifted man, but not, he himself recognised, a very good painter; the furniture and fabrics he designed at the Omega workshops were apt to be strangely hideous; and the decorations with which Vanessa Bell, Duncan Grant and their kin once covered the walls of a little Sussex church* have now a sadly amateurish air, and might very well have been mistaken for the efforts of the clergyman's own 'artistic' family. What really counts today is the contribution they made to the 'science of happiness', as Coleridge had once called it, by establishing a small coherent society that satisfied both their aesthetic sense of order and their ambitious conception of the good life. They were happily self-assured; had Bloomsbury produced Roger alone, it would have been as historically memorable as Athens in its greatest days, Virginia Woolf believed.

Their sense of superiority they did not trouble to conceal; and, as other self-sufficient groups have done, they made an individual use of language, and had a vocabulary and an intonation that were all their own; their voices were usually high-pitched, rising and falling and placing a dramatic emphasis on the most important words. '*Simply-Too-Extraordinary*' was the kind of epithet with which they characterised any theory or dogma, that, like the Christian faith in its more puritanical aspects, entirely passed their comprehension. But this did not preclude an eager appetite for knowledge. Roger Fry, whom the sheer 'extraordinariness' of the Old Testament (which he had not opened since his childhood) reduced to stentorian peals of laughter, on other subjects, wrote his admiring friend Clive Bell, displayed an 'occasionally nefast gullibility', now and then in his aesthetic judgements, but also in the value of certain queer patent medicines he enthusiastically recommended.

Even for a comparative outsider, observing the Bloomsburians, listening to their gossip and hearing their descriptions of one another, was always a memorable experience; they had the same ideals, which, of course, they might interpret variously, and the same conception of happiness, based both on personal and on intellectual relationships, that they preserved

* At Berwick, near Lewes. Cyril Connolly was buried in the churchyard.

until the end. Oddly enough, Leonard Woolf, after he had lost Virginia, though the most ascetic of them all, just as Clive Bell was the worldliest and most frivolous, seems in his last years to have been among the most contented; and I remember a meeting with Clive, not very long before his own death, at which he spoke of Leonard's solitary existence 'alone in the small country house where he had spent most of his troubled married life. Clive himself evidently much regretted the passing of youth, and, although he never grew openly melancholic, found his gradual attrition by old age, and the disappearance of his youthful pleasures, a more and more disheartening process. But he was warm-hearted, and had once, he told me, sympathetically enquired how Leonard, as a rule, began the day. With a feeling of expectation, Woolf replied; there were so many things to which he could look forward – his bath and his breakfast, the arrival of the postman and the latest *Times*, and then, accompanied by his devoted dog, a leisurely walk around the garden. Clive could not refrain from expressing his astonishment. 'I do believe, you old wretch,' he had commented, 'you're really a *happy* man, aren't you?'

Modern Bloomsbury is now once again a fairly prosaic London neighbourhood; and its inhabitants could hardly compare themselves to the citizens of ancient Athens. The original Bloomsburians have had no legitimate successors. Today the art of good talking, and, indeed, of appreciative listening, which has done so much to found friendships and thus promote happiness, seems to have fallen into a temporary decline. In Samuel Johnson's period, an ability to talk well was so important a part of social life that a somewhat taciturn man attracted unfavourable notice. Mrs Thrale, for instance, had an elderly friend who, besides being fat and slow, would occasionally stammer.

'Of Colonel Boden's conversation [she remembered in her *Anecdotes*] I . . . heard Johnson say that it reminded him of the Aloe Tree; that blossoms once in a hundred years & whose Shoot is attended with a cracking Noise resembling an Explosion; when that is over all is quiet till the return of the periodical Effort.'

A famous talker, of course, need not be a professional performer; and I doubt if we should now always enjoy hearing Sydney Smith – 'the loudest

wit' to whom Byron said he had ever had to listen – weave his elaborate conversational tapestries, or Macaulay, who, another critic remembered, 'not only overflowed with learning, but stood in the slop', discourse for the benefit of Lady Holland's guests. Table-talk at Holland House, though said to have been brilliant and discursive was, no doubt, a little studied. During the mid-Victorian Age, it was the splendid spontaneity of Tennyson's outbursts that once delighted Jane Carlyle. The time was January 1845; and she was alone, having made up her mind 'for a nice long quiet evening of *looking into the fire*', when a carriage drew up and she heard the sound of men's voices:

'. . . The men proved to be Alfred Tennyson of all people and his friend Mr Moxon . . . Alfred is dreadfully embarrassed with women alone . . . for he entertains at one and the same moment a feeling of almost adoration for them and an ineffable contempt . . . The only chance of my getting any right good of him was to make him forget my womanness – so I did just as Carlyle would have done – get out *pipes* and *tobacco* – and *brandy and water* – with a deluge of *tea* over and above – The effect of these accessories was miraculous – he *professed* to be *ashamed* of polluting my room . . . but he smoked on all the same – for *three* mortal hours! – talking like an angel – only exactly as if were talking with a clever man . . .'

When Tennyson had at last bidden her goodbye, and Carlyle, who had finally returned, found his wife sitting alone 'in an atmosphere of tobacco so thick that you might have cut it with a knife, his astonishment was considerable!' For the poet, despite his imaginative meanderings and chase of will-o'-wisps that would perhaps one day get him into trouble, the historian had always had a deep respect; and, much later, in his correspondence with Emerson, he portrayed both Tennyson's impressive physiognomy and his vigorous conversational style:

'. . . A man solitary and sad . . . dwelling in an element of gloom, – carrying a bit of Chaos about him . . . which he is manufacturing into Cosmos! . . . One of the finest-looking men in the world. A great shock of rough dusty-dark hair; bright-laughing hazel eyes; massive aquiline face, most massive yet most delicate . . . His voice is musical metallic, –

fit for loud laughter and piercing wail and all that may be in between; speech and speculation free and plenteous . . .'

Tennyson, Carlyle concluded, was indeed 'a true human soul, or some authentic approximation to it'; and I feel sure that, if the sage had lived on to witness the arrival of Oscar Wilde, the most magnetic talker of the late-Victorian Age, he would have found little to applaud either in the quality of the brilliant Irishman's soul or in his peculiar mode of self-expression. For a student of the present subject, however, Wilde's character and the history of his life seem to have a lasting interest. Happiness, his biographer assures us,* was his natural element; and there is no doubt he made his friends happy, and, as a speaker, delighted every audience he faced – whether they were a gang of American miners, whom, it is said, he could also sometimes drink under the table, or the cultivated frequenters of a London drawing room, whom their hostess had attracted by inscribing the words *'to hear Mr Oscar Wilde tell a tale'* at the bottom of her card.

He generously shared his own enjoyment of life. Yet no man with such an abundance of personal resources, to which he added a large share of executive, if not imaginative gifts, could have more deliberately squandered them; and this he did, not merely by ill-chance – his calamitous involvement in a savage family dispute – but through a perverse determination he had already formed at the height of his prosperity and fame. To fulfil his own genius, of which he was firmly convinced, he must at length adopt a tragic rôle. In 1895, when he entered his fourth decade and was travelling around Algeria, he met an enquiring young Frenchman, André Gide. His duty, Gide heard him say, should now be 'to amuse himself terribly'. It was not happiness he sought but pleasure; 'one must always desire what is most tragic'.

Yet, even after he had accomplished his social downfall, survived disgrace and imprisonment, written *De Profundis*, his lamentable apologia, in which he pretended that, as soon as he had emerged from gaol, he would become a solitary wanderer and 'seek clefts in the rocks where I may hide, and secret valleys in whose silence I may weep undisturbed', something at least of all his old 'invincible happiness' helped to support him through the years of exile. His letters at this period, where he describes, for instance, the

* Hesketh Pearson: *The Life of Oscar Wilde*, 1946.

rapacious yet attractive 'little friends' he frequently picked up on the boulevards, are among the most engaging that he ever wrote. His wit had kept its early edge; and, although the wounds inflicted by 'that tiger, Life', were now evidently past healing, he retained his kindliness and good humour. Those were the qualities that his remaining friends – two of whom, Ada Leverson, the golden-hearted 'Sphinx', and the veteran novelist Mrs Belloc Lowndes, I was lucky enough to meet before they died – spoke of with particularly deep affection; and Mrs Belloc Lowndes recollected his delicately understanding treatment of a tedious clergy-man's wife he and Mrs Wilde had once entertained at Tite Street. When she confessed that she was terrified of shipwrecks, he did his ingenious best to amuse and, at the same time, reassure her. On his own travels, he said, he invariably took with him his private hencoop that, used as a life-raft if the vessel sank, would always ensure him a safe passage home.

15

'Happy the Man'

SHOULD one suddenly notice that a picture one admires on a friend's wall hangs perhaps a quarter of an inch askew, the temptation to set its position right grows sometimes almost irresistible. This may well displease its owner; and the habit of meddling with and readjusting objects has, now and then, been diagnosed as a perverse neurotic trait. I remember hearing that, when a young man I knew visited an eminent psychiatrist, and his hand strayed towards some pencils strewn across the desk, his adviser, giving the slight smile of a satisfied expert, murmured 'Yes, yes, definitely *obsessive!*' while he made a rapid note upon his pad.

I prefer to think, however, that this odd tendency may have a much less morbid origin. In our general pursuit of happiness, does it not suggest our longing to give our existence a truly harmonious pattern, and substitute a sense of symmetry and equipoise for one of conflict and disorder? Thus, a poet whose art depends so much on balance and rhythm, but whose personal life, like that of Baudelaire, may be notably disordered, will often find that certain images have an especially deep imaginative appeal. 'The sober and elegant beauty' of a nineteenth-century sailing ship, Baudelaire wrote, was 'derived . . . from its regularity and symmetry which, in the same degree as complication and harmony, are among the primordial requirements of the human spirit . . .'. These splendid vessels, so calmly balanced on the waters, are they not asking us a silent question: '*Quand partons-nous pour le bonheur?*' When shall we set sail for happiness?

Any image that reconciles us both to our discordant selves and to the chaotic world in which we live, may make the expedition less difficult; and a modern Italian dramatist introduces a character who, despite an appalling physical flaw, is still so nearly happy that he clings to life, he tells

us, 'like a creeper to an iron railing'. Pirandello's play is entitled *The Man with a Flower in his Mouth*; and the 'flower' that blemishes the chief character's face, a small, perpetual spot, is the symptom of a disease that will, he knows, soon return and kill him. Meanwhile, his chief source of happiness – indeed, his only relaxation – is every evening to watch through a shop-window the girls measuring out lengths of ribbon and men expertly tying up parcels. For hours at a time he follows their operations:

> 'They pick up . . . a large sheet of double-thickness paper . . . Then with the back of the hand . . . they bring up one edge of the paper from underneath. Then they bring the other down – and so deftly, so gracefully, make the narrowest of folds . . . one they don't really need . . . put in, as it were for the sheer love of the art.'

His observation of a commonplace task skilfully performed gives Pirandello's hero as much happiness as, on another plane, he might have experienced from watching the creation of an aesthetic masterpiece, and that, as a picture or a piece of music would have done, quickens his spirit and strengthens his desire to live. But his consolation is transitory; the window will grow dark, the assistants disappear; and writers who describe the effects of happiness and the different forms it takes – which range from a sudden shaft of elation to a longer-lasting glow of pleasure – have also dwelt on its mortal transience and on the regrets its passing leaves behind.

In a song for a Christmas masque called *The Vision of Delight*,* written by Ben Jonson for James I's luxurious court, these nostalgic feelings are memorably recorded:

> 'We see, we heare, we feele, we taste,
> We smell the change in every flowre,
> We only wish that all could last,
> And be as new still as the houre'

Towards the end of the same century, however, a yet greater poet, John Dryden, introduced an equally moving but much less melancholy theme, which he had freely adapted from an ode by Horace.† The Past, both the

---

* Presented at Whitehall in 1617.
† '*The twenty-ninth Ode of the third Book . . . Paraphras'd in Pindaric Verse . . .*'

Roman and the English poet assert, is a treasure-house over which Memory, Mother of the Muses, should sit perpetually on guard:

'Enjoy the present smiling Hour;
And put it out of Fortune's Pow'r . . .
Happy the Man, and happy he alone,
He who can call to-Day his own:
He who, secure within, can say
To-Morrow do thy worst, for I have liv'd to-Day,
Be fair, or foul, or rain, or shine,
The Joys I have possess'd in spite of Fate are mine.
Not Heav'n itself upon the past has Pow'r;
But what has been, has been, and I have had my Hour.'

Every speculative and imaginative human being has his own attitude towards the past, and attaches a different value, in terms of happiness or misery, to the experiences he has gone through. While some, like Byron, cherish romantic regrets, others, like Coleridge's mariner, carry around with them an albatross-load of guilt, and still others, when they grow older, and less and less hopeful, acquire a philosophic detachment that enables them to see the vicissitudes through which they have travelled as details of the same not necessarily harmonious but possibly inescapable pattern. Such a view of life was expressed in the nineteenth century by Scrope Davies, one of Byron's closest early friends, but during his autumnal years a broken-down dandy, whose last refuge was a hayloft perched above a Belgian stable. In 1828, four years after the poet's death, he wrote to Francis Hodgson, another of Byron's old friends, thanking him for a particularly welcome letter:

'Your letter has recalled to my mind scenes the recollection of which now constitutes my only delight. Bacon somewhere observes: "Aristotle saith the young may be happy by hope, so why should not old men and sequestered men by remembrance?" The past and the future are the sole object of man's contemplation. There is no present, or if there is, it is a point on which we cannot stand. While I am now writing the future becomes the past. Happiness then is a pursuit, not an attainment.'*

* *The Life and Times of Scrope Beardmore Davies*, 1981.

[184]

Scrope Davies was by no means a professional writer, though a sensible and well-read man; and one of the functions of an imaginative artist, he would have agreed, is to hold a balance between the present and the past, and from what he has once felt and observed and his quotidian experience of life build up an intelligible scheme. Every writer is to some extent haunted by the memories of his youth; Dickens, for example, was so dominated by his recollections of his unhappy London childhood that there were certain streets, which, although he describes them with extraordinary vividness, as a successful middle-aged novelist he admitted that he could hardly bear to enter. In our own century Proust and Colette gazed back to past times even more keenly and sensitively than they looked around them at the present day. But there was one essential difference between the two great novelists, who made so large a contribution to the modern art of writing, and who, moreover, liked and knew one another well. Each had had a happy childhood – Proust at the little country town he rechristened Combray, which forms the background of *Du Côté de chez Swann*, where stood Tante Léonie's 'old grey house' and the medieval church that 'slipped its belfry into every corner of the sky'; Colette at the Burgundian home of her beloved mother Sido, from whom she inherited both her deep affection for all natural things and some of the basic virtues that were to carry her through a long adventurous bohemian career.

Only in Proust's opening volumes, however, does he portray either lasting happiness or genuine goodness; and the second quality is almost always reserved for the mother he adored but who sometimes disappointed him, or for his grandmother, Madame Amédée, a nineteenth-century disciple of Rousseau, who in their garden is constantly doing her best to restore the air of romantic wildness that their gardener so much dislikes, and who will now and then quietly remove an enclosing stake, so that the roses should look 'a little more natural', just as a mother might run her hand through her boy's hair, after the barber had smoothed it down, to allow it to stick out properly around his head.

Otherwise, except for these loving and lovable figures, while Proust's majestic journey into the past proceeds, illusion after illusion vanishes, and even the traits he had once admired in a character develop a very different and far uglier meaning. Thus, Robert de Saint-Loup, the aristocratic young cavalryman to whom the narrator had once attributed a genuine nobility of heart and mind, undergoes, as he enters middle age, a strange

and saddening transformation. He had still 'the grace and ease of a cavalry officer; but his swift-footedness was now generated by the fear of being seen and by the self-dissatisfaction and boredom' that dog him through his clandestine sexual life.

Before Proust had done with his characters only three of them remain permanently admirable – the painter Elstir, the novelist Bergotte and the composer Vinteuil; for all are selflessly devoted to the difficult art they practise; and through art alone, Proust came to believe, could he establish the mystic relationship he sought between the present and the past. Colette, on the other hand, though she might deal harshly with an individual character, had a deep regard for life itself, which extended to the whole creation. It was not enough to say, wrote Maurice Goudeket, her gifted third husband and the devoted guardian of her later years, that Colette loved animals. 'Before every manifestation of life, animal or vegetable, she felt a respect that was akin to a religious fervour.' And, at the same time, she was deeply conscious of the unity of the natural world 'in its infinite variety of shapes'. Hence the peculiar moving effect that her literary images produce: 'one doesn't read Colette', said a contemporary critic; 'one sees what she sees. One breathes in what she breathes; one touches what she touches'; and, since her senses are more delicately attuned than her reader's, 'he finds himself, for a few hours, living an intensified life', as though he were 'an ordinary violin . . . suddenly transformed into a Stradivarius'.*

If an affection for the world, and the ability to convey that affection, be an index of happiness, Colette, though life had often treated her roughly, and she had broken most of its social and moral rules, and suffered some unpleasant consequences, was indeed a happy woman; and her sympathetic attitude towards Nature was often reflected both in her letters and in her conversation. At our only meeting† she spoke of her single visit to England, and of a stream she had noticed wandering through a garden. Her visit must have taken place at least forty or fifty years earlier; but, thanks to

---

* Jean Larnac: *Colette, sa Vie, son oeuvre*, 1927; quoted by Joanna Richardson: *Colette*, 1983.
† See *The Wanton Chase*, 1980.

the tenderness of her phrase - '*une assez aimable petite rivière*' – the brooklet seemed to flow again.*

While writers of talent repeatedly disagree, genius will often respond to genius; and, despite their dissimilarity both as artists and as human beings, Colette had quickly recognised in Proust one of the greatest writers of their age. When the first volume of *A la Recherche du Temps Perdu* arrived, she became 'passionately attached to it'; they began to correspond, and from that day the appearance of a new Proustian volume was an important event in her life that induced her to put aside all other reading. This declaration, during the course of an interview with a literary editor, she made in 1925; and Proust had died on November 18th, 1922, leaving behind him, stacked around his comfortless room, a huge accumulation of proofs and manuscripts, all heavily amended and corrected. The last passage, dictated to his faithful servant, Céleste, he considered 'very good'. But now he must stop, he said: 'I can't do any more.'

Colette herself, crippled with arthritis but, as a rule, very much aware of life, survived him until August 1954. Only after her eightieth birthday did her mental energy show signs of flagging; she appeared slowly to lose touch with the present day; and on the afternoon of August 3rd, after long spells of semi-consciousness, she spoke her memorable last words, which Maurice Goudeket, in his loving tribute to his wife's genius, has recorded for our benefit.† They were accompanied by a wide embracing gesture that drew his attention to all the delightful details that surrounded them – the cases of brilliant Brazilian butterflies that were hung around her bed, her illustrated travel-books and her collection of nineteenth-century glass paper-weights, each with its own fantastic pattern – and simultaneously to a flight of sharp-winged swifts from the gardens of the Palais Royal that swept back and forth across her window. '*Regarde!*' she exclaimed, 'only *look*, Maurice!' It was a command she had issued again and again to her readers in almost everything she wrote.

---

* From a letter written to the poetess, Anna de Noailles, in 1928, I have copied an even more evocative passage: 'It's raining very gently and feels very good on the face and in the eyes. The entire park is starred with the white behinds of rabbits . . .'
† In *Près de Colette*, 1956.

Epilogue

IF this book has a single recurrent theme (which I may perhaps have over-emphasised) it is that, although happiness has many diverse forms, a particularly precious kind is often to be achieved not so much through a purposeful *'chasse au bonheur'* as through quietly observing and enjoying. 'The only thing in all my experience I cling to', the painter Walter Sickert told his young disciple Nina Hamnett, 'is my coolness and leisurely exhilarated contemplation. . .'. She must adopt the same attitude. 'Let this advice be my perpetual and most solemn legacy to you.'* Sickert's counsels were not intended for painters or poets alone; they apply, in some degree, to all mankind, even to Bertrand Russell's readers, whom he taught to 'feel themselves citizens of the universe, enjoying freely the spectacle it offers and the joys that it affords', thus reaching a 'profound instinctive union with the stream of life . . .' The exhilarated contemplation that Sickert recommended may be applied both to nature and to art; and not long ago I saw its effect on a well-known modern poet, who had a wide knowledge of art, but, apparently for the first time, had just come face to face with a famous work of classic sculpture.

It is one of a group of four statues that many other artists have loved and sometimes represented in a picture. Thus in Carpaccio's delightful vision of Saint Augustine meditating at his desk, while his little dog admires him from below, a medieval astrolabe hangs over the saint's head; but on the shelf that bisects the opposite wall more unexpectedly stand the statuette of a naked Venus and a miniature reproduction of one of San Marco's

* Quoted by Cyril Connolly: *The Unquiet Grave*, 1944.

St Augustine's little dog, from Carpaccio's painting in the *Scuola Dalmata dei S.S. Giorgio e Trifone* at Venice.

glorious Golden Horses. Although these familiar aspects of the Venetian scene have had a long eventful history, their origin is still mysterious; for, whereas some scholars attribute them to the fourth century BC, others believe that they may have been modelled and cast after the second century AD, during the dusk of Roman civilisation – a theory that would make their classic splendour even more remarkable. Rarely have masterpieces been so often stolen. The Emperor Constantine, who had acquired them no one knows how, set them up as ornaments of the Hippodrome at Constantinople; but the Doge Dandolo, leader of the Crusade that in 1204 conquered and plundered the imperial city, carried them away to Venice. There, however, they did not receive an immediately warm welcome; and for fifty years they were stored in the Arsenal until their value – should they

The Golden Horses of San Marco.

be melted down for cannon? – had been successfully decided; and they were raised on the façade of San Marco to the noble position that they hold today. Napoleon, of course, was the last plunderer. He included them in the loot of his Italian campaigns; and between 1797 and 1815 they framed the principal entrance of the Tuileries.

Since they were restored to San Marco, they have seldom been removed;

but in 1979 one of them (the second to the left of the team) briefly appeared in London for a Venetian Exhibition. There it was given the separate room it deserved; and among the crowd it drew I caught sight of my old friend John Betjeman. He was growing infirm, half crippled by the paralytic disease that had already confined him to a wheelchair; but from his chair, I saw, he was gazing up at the Horse's burnished beauty, at its proudly arched neck and majestic brazen flanks, in a state of silent rapture, which absorbed him completely, and no doubt had excluded for a while all ideas of age and illness. As the only gifted Poet Laureate since Tennyson, whose poems often sold no less readily than Byron's most romantic eastern Tales, John led an enviable literary life. But even at the height of his career, I remember thinking, he could have had few happier moments.

Index